KU-275-676

SCOTTISH HARD Bastards

SCOTTISH HARD Bastards

Jimmy Holland
with
Stephen Richards

JOHN BLAKE

Published by John Blake Publishing Ltd,
3, Bramber Court, 2 Bramber Road,
London W14 9PB, England

www.blake.co.uk

First published in hardback in 2006

ISBN 1 84454 242 4

All rights reserved. No part of this publication may be reproduced,
stored in a retrieval system, or in any form or by any means, without the
prior permission in writing of the publisher, nor be otherwise circulated in
any form of binding or cover other than that in which it is published and
without a similar condition including this condition being imposed on
the subsequent publisher.

British Library Cataloguing-in-Publication Data:

A catalogue record for this book is available from the British Library.

Design by www.envydesign.co.uk

Printed in Great Britain by William Clowes Ltd, Beccles, Suffolk

1 3 5 7 9 10 8 6 4 2

Text copyright © Jimmy Holland with Stephen Richards

Papers used by John Blake Publishing are natural, recyclable products
made from wood grown in sustainable forests. The manufacturing processes
conform to the environmental regulations of the country of origin.

Photographs: Mirrorpix (p2, top and bottom; p6, top left; p7, all; p8, bottom);
all others courtesy of Crimebiz.

Dedication

For those who died behind bars

CONTENTS

PROLOGUE

This book will take you deep inside the rough, mad, bad, drug-infested, cut-throat, back-stabbing world of Scottish-born, -bred, -raised or -adopted sons like no other book has done before or, for that matter, will ever do again: that is a promise. The sheer violence on these pages will chill your blood to the bone and will make the hairs on your neck stand on end.

You will find *explosive violence* such as coshings, scaldings, slashings (a typical Scottish favourite), stabbings, riots, hostages and, of course, ultimately, murders – some of which even took place within the fences and walls of the Scottish penal system.

I make no apologies for glorifying or lionising the characters that I have written about within these pages. They each have their reasons for the way in which the cookie crumbled either for or against them and who am I to stand in judgment against them? Unless you have been in their position, it is impossible to cast the first stone.

Although I may say that a particular character is a great guy, do not let that fool you into thinking that you, as a member of the public, could approach them: I have served my apprenticeship in the hate factories alongside some of them; I have gained their respect, friendship or simply just a knowledge of them by virtue of my own distasteful past. Therefore, do not be fooled by how I put them across in my own terms.

Because of some of the characters within the Scottish penal system, and as a result of their unbridled violence, hundreds of people have lost their lives and untold thousands have been scarred for life.

Many of the characters I have known are now dead; needless to say, the majority of them succumbed to violent deaths. That is how deep my connections go.

A handful of characters that I have never met have also been mentioned within these pages. I have deemed these particular men worthy of inclusion as a result of what I have heard about them over time. In addition, there are some men who I have had to omit from the book, as they are still too actively involved in crime to want to be exposed.

It is not my intention to reveal things about people that could lead to their imprisonment. Let me get one thing straight. Where things of an incriminating nature are mentioned, it is because such information is common knowledge, despite the fact that it would be difficult to prove in a court of law.

I have selected the *crème de la crème* of the toughest, maddest, hardest Scottish bastards that have ever drawn breath, from the tens of thousands of criminals I have mixed with behind bars, in the streets and who I have known of over the last three decades of my criminally active life – the eighties, nineties and noughties.

The men included in this book are not listed in order of hardest: each is different and have been chosen based on my own criteria. There is no attempt to match any one against the other or to stir up trouble by having missed certain characters who some believe should have made it through to my final choice. For any of the characters who have been left out simply because they have not come to my attention, I apologise.

These hard men cannot be compared to each other – some fight with their bare hands, some with their brains and others with weapons. Some have a sixth sense for survival and avoid death with catlike ease. I don't include any world champions at this or that, but I do include men who could wipe the floor with any world champion of anything you threw at them. The only sport some of these men among men know is pain; they have the ability to dish out pain beyond your wildest nightmares. As for size, remember – sometimes, less is more: a smaller area to hit, a smaller size to spot and far less time to see who is coming at you from out of the shadows.

On the other hand, take Brian Cockerill or 'The Taxman'. He's a mammoth with brainpower: an unstoppable force and a weapon of mass destruction with a megaton load in just one fist... he is truly awesome. He has been arrested literally hundreds of times, is suspected by the police of having been involved in half a dozen murders and has been arrested on as many murder investigations, but he always seems to walk away uncharged. No man would want to be on the receiving end of the Taxman's no-holds-barred punishment.

Cunning can be just as effective as size. Take James Crosbie. He was once classified as the most dangerous man in Scotland and became notorious for his daring bank robberies and for the way he managed to escape on a bicycle. He was the criminal mastermind behind many successful crimes carried out throughout the UK.

Everything about James Crosbie oozed gold-plated panache; even his flying-club membership number with the Glasgow Flying Club was akin to the James Bond image that he lived. He was a flamboyant, larger-than-life, fun-loving character, who loved guns, women and fast cars and who was considered a lovable rogue by those in the media.

Dubbed 'Lucky Jim', Crosbie stirred up a hornet's nest in the Scottish justice system after he was accidentally granted bail after he had been charged with robbery and attempted murder. In a fatal error of judgment, Glasgow sheriff court freed Crosbie from Barlinnie Prison. However, he enjoyed only a few minutes of freedom before the Scottish police zoomed in on the prison to re-arrest him on further bankrobbery charges.

Joe Boyle is a spectacularly violent man; most of the prison system doesn't seem to like Joe, but that is their problem. Yes, sir, Joe is one dangerous customer: he had only been out of prison for four days when he murdered a rival gangster who used to laugh at him when he was a kid.

Dingus McGee was in his early forties when he received

a life sentence with a twenty-year recommendation for his part in a cash-and-carry robbery that went horribly wrong: he blew the guard's brains out.

Each man has a story to tell and each of these stories could fill a book of their own. It just goes to show the impossible task of telling all that there is to tell. Perhaps the stories that don't make it into these pages will find their way into another book, and good luck to the prospective authors if that happens.

I am going to bring the infamous incidents that have taken place behind bars and on the streets over the past fifty years back to life like no other book has done before. If you enjoy true crime, then this book is definitely the one for you. The danger and the extreme violence that goes on inside the Scottish system – and on the outside – really is explosive. I hope you enjoy this book as much as I have enjoyed writing it, with my good friend and number one investigative author, Stephen Richards.

I just hope that the following stories don't give you nightmares or encourage you to commit any crimes.

Yours,
Jimmy Boy Holland. Respect.

INTRODUCTION

Just before I take you into the main part of this book, I would like to give you a quick intro to some of the prisons in Scotland. I don't want to hold you back from the rest of the book, but I feel it is important to give a Jimmy Boy Holland prisons rating.

The A to S of Scottish Prisons

Aberdeen	aka Craiginchess	Full of sheep shaggers, the jail smells, bad jail to do time in. 4/10.
Barlinnie	aka Big House	Biggest prison in Scotland, on average five or six slashings every week. Bad jail. 10/10 for violence.
Carstairs	aka Slipper Factory	State hospital. 8/10 for being mad as it gets.

Cornton Vale	aka Fannyhill	The only women's prison in Scotland.
Castle Huntly	aka Castle	7/10 because it runs a methadone programme.
Dungavel	semi-open	Now holds illegal immigrants for Scotland.
Dumfries	aka Vietnam	Most violent young offenders. 10/10 for violence.
Friarton	aka Butt sniffer	Bit of a holiday camp. 3/10
Glenochil	aka The Hills	Worst jail for screws, worst segregation unit. 6/10.
Greenock	aka Gateside	Lifers go there at end of sentence, quiet prison. 1/10 for being so boring.
Inverness	aka Porterfield	Where the infamous cages were. 4/10 for packing them in like sardines.
Kilmarnock	aka Bovrilsweet	Like a drugs factory, all mad with drugs, but good jail to do time. 8/10.
Longriggend	aka LRU	Now shut down. 8/0 for it ending in this way.
Lowmoss	aka The Ranch	Full of dafty's thirty-day shots, good jail for doing time. 10/10.

Noranside	Open prison	Holiday camp. 2/10.
Perth	No nickname	More likely to be murdered in this prison than in any other. Oldest prison in Scotland. 10/10 for violence.
Peninghame	Open prison	Now shut down.
Polmont	Young offenders	(YOI) Liked it so much, I had to keep going back to this hate factory. 10/10.
Peterhead	aka The Napper	Full of beasts now and no cell-sharing. Not like it used to be. 6/10.
Saughton	aka Chavi ville	Easy time for relaxation. 10/10.
Shotts	aka Little Iraq	Worst jail for riots in Scotland. 10/10 for violence.

Note: The infamous special units at Barlinnie, Peterhead and Shotts have now been shut down, as have the notorious cages at Inverness.

Here is a clear guide to Scotland's prison system and to the hardest bastards ever to have been housed within it, scrapped within it, celebrated and forgotten inside it. Scotland's population at the last census was 5.7 million. Out of that number, 17,000 are constant offenders.

However, there are only 6,153 spaces in Scotland's twenty prisons and that number was reduced by 700 when three of those prisons shut down. This places a lot of pressure on the remaining prisons. Barlinnie has more prisoners per head of population passing through it than any other prison in Europe.

Most prisons in Scotland are overcrowded: the cramped atmosphere causes the tension inside the prison to build and build before it explodes into violence.

The Scottish prison system has the highest rate of suicides per head of population as well. Most of these poor people were petty criminals who never should have been sent to prison in the first place. Some of them suffered from undetected mental illnesses.

I would like to mention Shotts Prison for just a brief moment. There has been a prison in Shotts village since the early 1970s. E-Hall was opened for local Lanarkshire prisoners and held a maximum of sixty prisoners. Then someone in power decided to extend the prison into a 550-capacity, state-of-the-art, showpiece jail. It took over three-and-a-half years to build.

Once it opened, it was the first prison in Scotland – apart from Greenock – to have sinks and toilets in the cells. Still, a major riot took place there within the first year and no one could have predicted just how violent the new Shotts prison would have become: it has one of the worst records of violence in the full Scottish penal system! If they could have predicted that, they would never have built the extension in the first place.

I would just like to take a minute from this chapter to

send my condolences to all those who have lost a loved one in prison. I lost a very close friend and co-accused to suicide myself. I know what you must be going through. May every last one of you Rest in Peace. May God look upon you with love and warmth. To the lost children of Scotland. Love and Respect. Yours, Jimmy Boy Holland.

1

Solitary Dangermen

MALKJE LEGGAT

What I am about to tell you is not fiction; these are all real-life hard bastards who have a strong desire for blood and guts. I am going to start this chapter with my friend Malkie (Malcolm) Leggat, a convicted killer who once led a five-day prison riot.

I first heard Malkie's name when I was a fresh-faced young offender. So young, in fact, that my face was still covered in acne. I would go as far as to say that I was still wet behind the ears. Even back then, Malkie's name kept popping up like some sort of superstar's until, one day, my curiosity got the better of me. I started to ask some of the older boys in the young offenders (Young Offenders' Institute) why Malkie's name kept being flung around so regularly.

One of the top boys, Aldo Aitkenhead, who I didn't really know at that time, but who went on to make quite a name for himself in prison – I'll tell you more about him later – told me the story about Malkie.

Malkie had just been in Scotland's worst-ever prison riot and hostage war. In September 1987, at Peterhead Jail in the northeast of Scotland, just one year into the life sentence he had received at Glasgow High Court in August 1986 for killing twenty-three-year-old James Sweeney outside a Glasgow hotel, Malkie and his good friend Sammo took the prison warden, Jackie Stewart, hostage at knifepoint. On another occasion, Malkie, a staunch football fan, stabbed two prison officers after they refused to let him watch Rangers play in a European match... he received an extra three years for that.

Aberdeenshire's Peterhead Jail housed the hardest, baddest, meanest, motherfucker prisoners in the Scottish prison system. Because of this, no one was surprised when the pressure-pot jail finally erupted into a display of violence that has not been seen or equalled since.

After being taken hostage, the prison warden was in a very bad way, both mentally and physically. He had suffered beatings, starvation and humiliation. He had his key chain wrapped around his neck and was paraded around the jail's 90ft-high rooftop above D-wing like a dog. By this stage, the warden was a broken man: he sat with his hands on his knees, constantly wiping the tears of terror from his weather-beaten face.

Malkie didn't seem to give a fuck for human life and, as he had just been sentenced to life, had nothing to lose from his rampage of madness on the rooftop.

The siege went on for five days before the SPS lost total control, at which point they had no choice but to inform the government, which was, at the time, led by the Iron Lady – Margaret Thatcher.

Malkie and Sammo must have certainly got up their noses, because Thatcher instructed the most feared fighting force the world has ever seen to bring Malkie and his unstoppable gang to justice. Thatcher was at one of her biggest Conservative Party weekends and there, live on television, was Malkie, jumping around on the prison rooftops and threatening to smash Jackie Stewart's head in with a claw hammer before flinging him off the roof to his death.

Maggie was the only person in Britain who could give the SAS their direct orders to storm the prison and so, when negotiations broke down, the government's crisis management Cabinet group, Cobra, headed by the then-Home Secretary, Douglas Hurd, dispatched the SAS under the cover of darkness to rescue Jackie Stewart and to round up Malkie, Sammo and the rest of their little gang of troublemakers.

No one was expecting the six-man team of elite SAS soldiers to storm the prison, but that is exactly what happened. Hurling stun grenades and tear gas canisters, they entered the jail through a skylight and freed the terrified prison warder.

I have talked to most of the people that were involved and every single one of them has said that they didn't hear or see a thing. And when they did, it was too late!

The SAS flung flash bombs at Sammo, little Jake Devin and some of the others to blind them and to stun them for long enough to allow the men in black to take control of the hall. Jake was flung over the top flat balcony, some 40ft up, fell onto his back and was severely injured. The riot screws didn't give a monkey's about the state he was in. They dragged him by his hair into the first open cell and then proceeded to strip and beat him. Malkie was the last ringleader to surrender. He and Sammo were repeatedly coshed over their heads by the riot screws' batons, before being bundled into empty cells on the bottom flat of the hall. Once they were there, they received some of the worst beatings that have been dished out from the riot screws.

Once the screws left, most of the six or seven boys who had been overpowered by the SAS were in no fit state to move, never mind talk. In May 1988, Malkie, Sammo and one other boy received a total of twenty-seven years between them for mobbing, rioting and assault. Malkie had a total of twelve years added to his sentence and was ordered to spend two-and-a-half years in total solitary. After he had done that, he was moved to HMP Shotts and wasted no time in getting his own back on the screws.

One day, Malkie walked into their office and pulled out a lock-back knife. The screws froze on their chairs, before Malkie plunged the knife deep into their chests and bellies. After he had done it, he walked calmly out of the office and told the other boys in the section that he had just stabbed the hell out of two wardens.

One of the injured screws managed to raise the alarm before he fell onto the office floor. When he was finally taken to hospital, after having lost three pints of blood, it was discovered that the other warden wasn't as badly hurt as had first appeared.

Malkie was taken back down to the segregation unit, where he spent the next four-and-a-half years. On his release, the screws asked him whether he would like to go to the Shotts special unit, which had been opened in a blaze of glory back in 1991.

The unit housed the prisoners that the Scottish prison system couldn't handle – as much for their own safety as for the safety of the prison wardens and the other convicts. Once he was there, Malkie adapted to some normality: he didn't need to stab any more screws or cons; he was in a safe, controlled unit and he flourished, so much so that after three-and-a-half years, he left to go back into mainstream prison. This time, however, his head was screwed on the right way round.

Malkie was making good progress when he was moved onto Pentland Hall, down in HMP Saughton, and he got his tariff date of eighteen years – he had already served twenty years, but the system did not think that he was ready for release.

Nearing the end of his sentence, and still in a progressive move, he was being prepared for a move to an open prison when, in March 2005, he failed to return to Gateside Jail in Greenock while on a work community placement with, would you believe, the Salvation Army.

Ten weeks after he absconded, Malkie was captured in a slick operation when heavily armed police, backed by dog handlers and a force helicopter, swooped on him in Llanfaes, Anglesey, Wales. Unbelievably, Malkie had just moved in with a woman he had met only days after going on the run at a party.

With some luck, he can soon walk out of the prison gates a free man. He has done more than his fair share of time the hard way. On a scale of one to ten, Malkie is definitely a ten: his violence and his escapades are legendary within the prison system.

JOHN McPHEE

John McPhee also deserves a mention here. Released from Strangeways Prison in 1992 after serving time for robbery, he became a Scots mercenary and joined up with the Croatians, with whom, he readily admits, he committed the most sickening war crimes. His rap sheet reads like an intro to Attila the Hun: drug convictions, a suspect in thirteen murder cases and, at one time, on the UK's most wanted list. Read John's book, *The Silent Cry: One Man's Fight for Croatia in Bosnia*. It centres on his activities in the region as a volunteer solider of the HVO (Croat Defence Council). His involvement in the crisis in former Yugoslavia escalated following the death of his Muslim lover and her child – they were side by side when they died – and he returned from the Balkans both mentally, as well as physically, scarred.

`DINGUS´ McGHEE

Which leads me on to James 'Dingus' McGhee. He received a life sentence with a twenty-year recommendation for his part in a cash-and-carry robbery that went horribly wrong and resulted in him blowing a guard's brains out. The three other hardened criminals who carried out the robbery with Dingus turned Queen's Evidence against him at their High Court trial. In return, they all got four, six and nine years respectively for their parts in the robbery.

Dingus was a quiet man in prison. He didn't bother anyone and everyone liked him. He was in his early forties when he arrived at Shotts Prison and got camped up with some of the older cons he had done time with when he had been jailed in Peterhead for an earlier offence, before the jail turned into a perverts' prison. He didn't raise his voice in anger once at any warden or con and always went to work every day, from Monday to Friday. Most people that knew him would agree that Dingus is a total gentleman, though not someone to catch in a bad mood.

When the infamous Shotts riot of 1993 kicked off, Dingus was in the hall. However, he took no part in it whatsoever; he just sat in one of his friend's cells, smoked hash and waited for the riot to end. He had seen all the crazy shit before; he had been in Peterhead some years earlier when Malkie and Sammo had taken the hostage.

He didn't know it at the time, but two prison wardens had been badly stabbed, one of them in the lower back and legs, and couldn't walk. When the other prison warden saw that his friend had fallen to the ground, he went back in among a heavily armed masked gang of prisoners and tried to pull his friend to safety. He got stabbed in the arm and back for his trouble. Once the wardens had managed to seal the rampant cons in the hall, they went back to help their wounded colleague. The warden that had tried to save his friend didn't even know that he had been stabbed. Fair play to him: how many men do you know who would put their own life in danger to help pull a colleague to safety from a baying mob of hardened criminals? Not very many, is the answer. The screw in question got a bravery award for his actions.

The Shotts screws were used to this kind of occurrence, as there had been one major incident or another every year since the showplace jail opened back in 1978.

The screws were very pissed off by the fact that one of the cons had stabbed two of their pals and they promised revenge. When they finally got the hall back under control, some forty-three hours after it had started, they didn't waste any time in dishing out their own summary brand of justice. At first, every con was placed in his cell; some had two to a cell, others had three.

The first cell door to be opened after everybody had been locked up was Dingus'. They dragged him out and kicked and punched his face and body. After he had fallen to the floor, one nameless screw kicked him so hard between his legs that one of his balls became lodged in his belly, the other swelled to some six or seven times its normal size.

The riot screws did not stop there: they then dragged him down the corridor, where ten other nameless screws repeatedly coshed him over the head, face and body. Dingus was out cold by now, having received the injuries equivalent to someone who had been involved in a car crash. He received even more torture at the hands of the screws after he had been transferred to Barlinnie's tough segregation unit. I know their names, but for legal reasons I cannot name them; no one knew that Dingus had received a punctured lung during the beating and that his lung was filling up with his own blood – he was basically drowning in his own blood. He also had three fractures to his skull, two broken ribs and a smashed eye socket. He was dragged bodily into a silent cell, where he was stripped naked and left.

If you want to look to the medical profession for a true hard bastard, then, in my opinion, there is none 'harder' than the following man. I mean 99.9 per cent of doctors would want to protect their pension and keep in with the in-crowd. Not, however, this man among men. The star witness against the screws from Barlinnie was Dr Simon Danson; he also featured in a documentary about the brutality that prisoners had received during his three years of working in Barlinnie.

After Dr Danson had spoken out on a 1996 BBC television documentary about the violence used by prison officers against cons, the SPS subjected him to formal disciplinary charges for gross misconduct for having given the interview without permission. Dr Danson had made a series of claims about violent assaults on three prisoners by staff at Barlinnie and, as a result, three prison officers subsequently appeared in court charged with having assaulted inmates.

Although the SPS were trying to get back at Dr Danson,

the British Medical Association (BMA) supported him and promised to provide him with a vigorous defence of the gross misconduct charge. The BMA said: 'A doctor's first duty is to his patients and, although a prisoner loses liberty, he does not lose the right to a proper standard of medical and ethical care.'

After some wrangling, the SPS dropped all its charges against Dr Danson after he accepted an offer of voluntary severance.

Fair play to you, Doctor: you did the right thing, as the screws think they are a law unto themselves. In January 2005, Dr Danson wrote a paper for the Society of Prison Psychiatrists and raised some pretty poignant matters when he wrote:

> About fifteen years ago, I was working as a medical officer in a Scottish prison. I was learning the job and one of my duties was to attend when someone had hanged himself and to certify him dead.
>
> Of all the things I had to learn about prisons, the most distressing was the reaction of people to death. On one occasion, I was greeted with glee: 'One off the numbers, sir!' On another, I found a nurse standing with his foot on the dead man's chest and the ligature around his neck not completely removed. I regularly discussed problems with the other medical officers and mentioned my reaction to this. One of them answered: 'That's nothing – the screws used to put their cigarettes out in their ears!'

It was very distressing to have to deal with a series of assaults by staff upon inmates and I chose a method that eventually led to my leaving and moving to Wales, where I did not have this particular problem.

When Dr Danson encountered Dingus after his beating at Barlinnie, he turned away in disgust: he could not believe the state that Dingus had been left to lie in. He refused to treat him where he lay because he knew that Dingus's injuries were life threatening and told the top warden that Dingus would need to be rushed to Glasgow Royal Infirmary for emergency surgery. However, the screws in the seg block refused to listen to him; they pushed and manhandled their own doctor out of Dingus's cell and threatened him with a severe beating if he disclosed the cause of Dingus's injuries.

The doctor was having none of the screws' shit. He went straight up to see Barlinnie's top governor and told him about Dingus McGhee and his life-threatening condition. Upon hearing the doctor's side of the story, the governor instructed him to phone for an ambulance. Dingus was rushed by ambulance to Glasgow Royal Infirmary where he had life-saving surgery. If he had been left to lie in the cell for a couple of hours longer, he would almost certainly have died of his horrendous injuries.

Once the seg screws found out what Dr Danson had done, he was threatened and then shunned by all or most of the Barlinnie prison wardens. Wherever you are, Dr Danson, shine on.

The worst part of this story is that Dingus McGhee hadn't even been involved in the Shotts riot of 1993: the screws mixed up his name with that of Frank McPhee and it was he, rather than Dingus, who 'should' have received the injuries. What's more, Frank was well known in the prison system for being someone who caused as much trouble as he possibly could.

Frank was one of the gypsies; he was a tough man who had many years of violence behind him. In and out of prison, he had arranged the riot after the visit screws had strip-searched his boy's mother. Frank's boy was in the prison at the same time, although not many people knew that a man called Mark McClymont was Frank's son.

Anyway, Mark's mother was strip-searched for drugs while visiting, and that sent Frank into a wild frenzy. He was very pally with little Paul Sheenan from Paisley and little Rab Leslie from Port Glasgow. They may well have been small in stature, but these two young men were very dangerous in Shotts Prison at that time.

Frank, Paul and Rab are now dead: they were murdered after their release from prison. Frank was shot in the head by an IRA sniper outside his own front door in 2000. One shot was all that was needed; the killer was hiding away in a nearby tenement building – he left his rifle there after the shooting. It was a tit-for-tat killing; it was said that, after he had knifed a big face's son, McPhee had a bounty of £20,000 put on his head.

Rab had his throat cut: the boy who did it received five years. Paul was stabbed in the heart as he lay sleeping in his girlfriend's bed. The boy who did that received a life sentence.

These three men were responsible for the stabbing of the two screws during the riot. However, they all fell out with each other afterwards, as they all wanted the credit for the stabbings. In actual fact it was Paul who had performed the act and not Frank or Rab, as some people thought.

Some years after the riot, Frank and Dingus laughed about the incident; it wasn't a laughing matter at the time. Frank, Paul and Rab will feature more in this book in later chapters.

Dingus was held in total solitary for some three years after his return from hospital. I am glad to say that he pursued an action against the screws and the system and was awarded £20,000 in damages. The screws who had dished out the beatings stood in court charged with serious assault but, as always, the case against them collapsed.

Dingus is currently serving the rest of his twenty years down in Greenock's Christwell House. Hope you are plodding on, pal. Keep your chin up. Lots of respect mate. Yours, Jimmy Boy.

JOE BOYLE

As I've said, Joe Boyle is a violent man disliked by the prison system. There are people I am going to put in this book who I don't like either, but that doesn't mean that I don't recognise what they have done in the prison system – and you can't ignore hard bastards like these.

But Joe is my friend. He was, and still is, a deep person and someone who is difficult to get to know. Perhaps that is why people don't like him. The first time I met him, he was in the remand centre up in Longrigend, a place where one young boy thinks that he is the top man until some other young boy comes along and slashes his face off or stabs him up.

Joe had made a name for himself even back then. I have witnessed two or three boys trying to cosh and slash Joe, but he wasn't, and still isn't, anyone's mug. Joe picked up a pool cue and smashed it over the three boys' heads; he didn't stop until the screws pulled him off them. As a result of this sort of behaviour, Joe was always in the seg units.

When he was twenty-one years old, he became classed as an adult con and the crazy diamond set out on a one-man mission to take over Perth adult jail. And by fuck, he gave it a very good shot. Most of the so-called gangster hard men didn't want to know when Joe offered them a roll-about with his bare hands or with knives. Once, when Joe was sleeping in his bed, two men ran into his cell with knives in their hands and tried to murder him. However, Joe being Joe, and not giving two fucks about his own safety, ran at them head on in his cell. In fear, one dropped his knife and bolted; the other tried to stand his ground, but to no avail. Joe stabbed him.

I recall another incident when Joe was younger. A hard man by the name of Burnside used to hit him and his little brothers and sister. However, when Joe grew up, he waited until Burnside came to prison and evened the scores: he dragged the man kicking and screaming into his cell and proceeded to stab him in the eye. And that wasn't all. He then stuck a teaspoon into Burnside's damaged eye and scooped it out of the socket. Yes sir, Joe is one violent man.

He had only been out of prison for four days when he murdered a rival gangster who used to laugh at him when he was a kid. It was the first time that Joe had seen his rival in over ten years. He received a life sentence for his troubles and was put straight into the seg unit in Barlinnie, before being transferred to the Shotts man-eater, along with some forty or more other hardened prisoners who were doing their rules (segregation punishment) for their part in a riot or a hostage-taking or a stabbing or some other incident. The forty-odd prisoners teased and taunted Joe at the windows, day in, day out. They never did so to his face.

Joe made it his personal goal in life to go to war with every single one of them and that is exactly what he did. He would make sure that he got let out to use the phone; it was an excuse to catch whichever hard man was going to a visit that night – to get there, they had to walk past Joe when he was on the phone.

I can tell you because I was there: some of the so-called hardest men in the system cancelled their visits because they didn't want to have to face Joe. The screws and shrinks couldn't place Joe into mainstream prison, so they marked him down as insane and shipped him up to the state hospital for his own safety, and even more for the safety of the screws and the other cons.

I still write to Joe. He has now been up in the state hospital for twelve years, is doing really well and could soon be up for release. If Joe had been forced to do his time in a mainstream prison, among the cons, there would definitely have been a string of murders; that is how dangerous Joe was and still can be, but let's all hope that he can keep his cool. Joe, brother, you know that you have got so many good people around you now and that you don't need to go back down that slippery slope of pure and utter violence. I hope to see you very soon when you get out. Give Linda, Scott, Maria and the kids my love. Your friend till the end. Love and respect bro.

TOMMY GORDON

Tommy Gordon started off by doing three years in the young offenders'. He is still in prison, though, as he had a 'run-in' with another young offender during his stint there. I don't see eye to eye with this boy - but you cannot take it away from him, he is a dangerous bastard. It is common knowledge in prison that Tommy is a homosexual, but that doesn't bother me.

But what did bother me was that Tommy lied and in turn made me out to be some sort of liar, someone who went out of his way to embarrass him in front of his peers, such as Kenny Kelly (who had a name for himself in prison back in the good old Peterhead days, but I will go into that in more detail later).

Tommy took it upon himself to issue me with a

personal threat. He thought that because he had murdered a prisoner – by sticking an 18in knife through the boy's back and leaving it in – I was going to back down. Maybe some weaker people would have backed down, but I wasn't going to let this boy rule my life. I dealt with it by stabbing him, but this isn't my story, this is Tommy's.

As a result of murdering the young prisoner, Tommy and a boy called Raymie Holland both received life sentences and were sent to Dumfries young offenders. Tommy had ideas of making a break for freedom and that is what he did, along with a boy called Jacko.

They managed to escape from Dumfries top security young offenders and were away for over a week. Once they were caught, Tommy and Jacko lay rotting in the seg unit for some thirteen months before they got back up the stairs to mainstream prison.

Tommy was then sent to Glenochil adult prison. I soon followed in his footsteps and that is where I had my own run-in with him, sending him to hospital in the process. After his recovery, he moved on to Perth Prison, where he was the ringleader in some trouble that resulted in a screw being taken hostage.

He was placed back in seg units and received a further six years on top of his life sentence for the hostage incident, before being transferred to the newly opened Peterhead special unit. There he had a run-in with my friend and former co-accused, Billy Lewis.

Tommy stabbed Billy through the face with a lock-back knife, but was injured himself during the scuffle and was taken to the hospital in Peterhead. During the hospital transfer, he made good his escape from his prison guard escort.

Tommy was back on the run: he managed to stay out of prison for some six weeks, before he was eventually trapped in one of the main train stations down in London. After photos of him had been plastered all over the television and in the newspapers, a family from Scotland recognised him. How unlucky is that?

You see, even though I hate this boy, I still take my hat off to him for what he has done. He has never taken his sentence lying down, no sir. Tommy is, and always will be, a fighter to the very end. He has now been in prison for sixteen years and people tell me that if he keeps screwing the nut he could be up for release within four years. That must be a bonus for him and I wish him all the best for getting out of prison, even though I don't like him. He is still one of the most badass cons I have done my time with and I will close his story here.

`PORKIE´ O´ROURKE

James 'Porkie' O'Rourke is serving his life sentence down in Kilmarnock's privately run prison. He had been involved with me in various activities on a few different occasions and has also taken three hostages in his own right while serving out his life sentence.

Sadly, Porkie is still being held in prison. He would have been released back into the community if it wasn't for the fact that he is one of the most dangerous men in the Scottish prison system. Porkie received a further seventeen years on top of his life sentence for his part in the three incidents of hostage-taking.

When we were in Glenochil together, we were co-accused of having taken a warden and a prison nurse hostage at knifepoint for the contents of her medical bag.

We both had heroin habits of the injecting variety. It was just after New Year, all of our own drugs had run out and we needed to get drugs from somewhere and fast. Most other prisoners would have just given up the chase and accepted the fate of going through 'cold turkey'. However, we came up with what seemed like the ingenious plan of robbing the civilian doctor as he came on an emergency call with a bag full of drugs. However, nothing ever seems to go to plan; particularly when two desperado junkies have hatched it.

It was a Sunday afternoon. We had asked another one of the prisoners to pretend that he was ill. The nurse from the health centre came down to look at him and told him that she would need to go back up to the health centre to phone the doctor, who no doubt, would have been busy on the golf course or whatever else he did on a Sunday afternoon. One-and-a-half hours passed before the nurse came back down to the hall with her prison warden escort. She entered the cell, carrying her black leather surgery bag; a bag that contained all the drugs that other prisoners in the hall needed that night.

Porkie and I were standing in a cell opposite to the one in which the prisoner, the nurse and the warden were standing. Time was getting on and the last glimpses of daylight were quickly disappearing. It was 4.35pm when we heard the nurse telling the sick boy that the doctor wouldn't be able to attend on him until at least 5.30pm.

That was fine and dandy for the prisoner, but not for us. The hall was going to be locked up for the night at 4.55pm and we had no other option. We couldn't wait any longer, as the withdrawal symptoms were starting to take their toll on our bodies. We were pouring buckets of cold sweat, tears were running down our faces and, every time we yawned, the pain was so severe that words do not come close to describing it.

Anyone who has had a drug habit will know exactly what we felt like, but for those of you who have not, I can only try and explain. Imagine you had toothache all over your body, constantly. Added to that you have hot and cold sweats, you can't stand on the same spot for more than two seconds, you can't even hold down a cup of water in your belly without being sick, the shits run freely out of your rear end – you never have control of your own bowels – and your head feels as though someone was constantly smashing a cricket bat over it. All of that is happening to you at the same time. That is how Porkie and I felt that day. I am not telling you this to try and get your pity. No fucking way. I am simply trying to highlight the things that drug addicts have to go through every time their smack runs out. Perhaps it will give you a better insight as to why people on drugs do such dangerous and desperate things to get their hands on the money for the next hit that will take away the most horrible feeling in the world. Next time you see a junkie, stop for ten seconds and think back to what I have just told you: it may lead you to a glimmer of understanding about the things we do.

Anyway, Porkie and I agreed there and then to take the warden, the nurse and the prisoner hostage. Once we entered the prisoner's cell, the warden, who I shall keep nameless, protested that we shouldn't be there and asked us kindly enough to leave. It was far too late for any pleasantries.

I pulled out the homemade jail knife I had been holding in my hand; Porkie pulled out a very sharp lock-back knife that he had concealed up his sleeve. We told the warden and nurse to sit on the floor and that if they did as they were told them then no one would get hurt.

I will not go into details, but the warden put up some resistance – fair play to him – but we were so desperate for the drugs in the nurse's medical bag that nothing was going to stop us from getting them. We grabbed the bag of drugs from her hand; we were like two tramps round a bag of chips in a bin.

We hurriedly drank all the Valium and Mogadon juice, then we swallowed anti-psychotics as well, with not one care in the world for our own safety. Some of the psychotic drugs were 500 milligrams at a time, but none of that entered our minds (excuse the pun). Once we had drunk and popped all the pills worth popping in her bag, we sat on the cold cell floor until the highly dangerous cocktail of drugs kicked in.

Thirty minutes later, Porkie and I were rubber men: the screw and the nurse could easily have taken the knife from our hands when we slipped in and out of consciousness but they didn't; the hostage situation lasted until 11.30am the following morning, by which point Porkie and I were back to square one – rattling, strung out and with nowhere to go: we were trapped in a cell with a screw, a nurse and a prisoner. Outside in the section, there were about fifty riot screws and negotiators.

After coming to some sort of agreement with the screw and the nurse, Porkie and I gave ourselves up. I didn't see my friend Porkie again until we appeared at Edinburgh High Court, where we both got six years on top of our sentences – all for one night of madness. It just goes to show how drugs can get a grip over your mind.

Porkie went on to the Shotts unit and was doing great until he had a run-in with Billy Lewis, another one of my friends and co-accused. I will go into detail about our adventures together later. Porkie and Billy had been pally for some time in the unit and Billy, because he had a lot of family and friends on the outside who looked after him, kept Porkie's drug habit going. Porkie, on the other hand, was pretty much alone: his bird had called time on their relationship; his so-called pals didn't want to know him; and even his own father and sister had moved down to England.

Anyway, Porkie and Billy were really close. After all, they were in the Shotts special unit together. Only the hardest bastards, the worst of the worst prisoners, were placed in that unit; people who were a danger to themselves, to the screws and to the other prisoners alike.

Porkie was on a visit with some bird or other; it wasn't his own girlfriend as she had ended their affair. The bird got up and brought him some heroin. After he had come back off his visit back, Billy asked his friend if he had got any drugs. Porkie told Billy that he hadn't received a thing and the rest of the day, 24 December, passed by. When the prisoners in the unit went behind doors that night, Billy didn't have a clue that Porkie was going to give another prisoner some heroin. Billy got wind of what was happening, came to his window and asked Porkie where his square-up was. Porkie told his friend that there wasn't anything there for him.

Porkie had received a stash at his visit that he was supposed to share with a different prisoner in the special unit. Billy and Porkie started growling at each other through the windows and Billy ended up telling Porkie that he would sort the argument out the next morning, Christmas Day.

Billy didn't sleep at all that night: he was rattling, strung out and his mind was racing. When the screws came on shift the next day, they opened Porkie's cell door before they opened Billy's. By the time Billy left his cell, Porkie was already sitting up at the TV and video, watching some movie from the night before.

There was a really big, fuck-off steak knife sitting in the kitchen. When Billy was finally let out of his cell, he went into the kitchen, grabbed the knife and marched over to Porkie's cell. Of course, the cell was empty.

Fuming, Billy placed the knife up his sleeve and left Porkie's cell. He then spotted Porkie sitting watching the

TV and made his way over to him. Two or three screws were also sitting watching the video when Billy pulled out his knife and started stabbing Porkie in a mad, frenzied attack. I don't think he meant it, but Billy impaled Porkie's face onto the sofa: the knife had gone straight through Porkie's cheek, came out the back of his neck and had stuck into the wooden frame of the sofa. That was after Porkie had suffered three other stab wounds.

That, to me, is a really bad Christmas present, but to Porkie's credit, he never let out any screams or anything like that. He even pulled the knife out of the sofa's frame himself. Billy was removed to the segregation unit once again. Porkie went to hospital for emergency surgery to remove the kitchen steakie on Christmas Day.

You see, when you end up in the Shotts special unit or in the Peterhead special unit, you have to keep up the appearance of being just as hard as the next boy; if you don't, it won't be long until you are found out.

That is exactly what prison is like. When you read all these stories about jail being a holiday camp it makes me laugh out loud. I don't know one holiday camp in Britain where slashings, stabbings, gang warfare and murder is the norm. Do any of you? If so please get in contact with me, then I can go on holiday there to remind myself of what it was like for me behind bars.

After Porkie left the special unit down in Shotts he went to HMP Aberdeen Craiginchess, where he lasted some five weeks before he and another man took a warden hostage at knifepoint. The siege lasted some seventeen hours before they let the warden out.

Porkie went back to Perth segregation unit where he spent the next thirteen months. He also had another nine years added to his life sentence. I can truthfully say that my friend is a dangerous boy, indeed. Ask yourselves, for one minute, why do you think that boys like us do such nasty things in prison? I will tell you: it is a combination of the sentence, the drugs and the screws' sick attitudes.

ANDY McCANN

Andy McCann is another lifer, currently serving his sentence in Glenochil Prison, where he has been for the last eighteen months. Andy is no stranger to violence: he has dished out some nasty business to the screws in his time. He was a career criminal with a very tough reputation in his home town before he got sent down for murdering a rival gangster over a drug deal.

When Andy came to prison he wasn't very well liked: some saw him as a bully, others simply as a threat. When Andy walked into Shotts Prison, he was lured into a cell thinking that he was going to catch up with a friend. Once he got there it was too late. He couldn't leave and was savagely attacked by a group of cons.

The leader of the mob was Rab Leslie, who had had a run-in with Andy some years earlier. Andy stood his ground and went head to head with the four other prisoners, all of whom had homemade prison knives in their hands. He received a stab wound to his neck – it missed his jugular vein by millimetres – but, to give Andy his due, he stood on his own two feet and fought for his life. If he had fallen to the cell floor at any stage, there is no doubt that he would have been murdered.

Andy received some six stab wounds, three of them life threatening, before he managed to get back out of the cell. From there, he staggered to the screws' office, where he collapsed. Andy was rushed to nearby Law Hospital in a prison van; they couldn't wait for the ambulance... if they had, Andy wouldn't be here today.

None of the boys who carried out the attempted murder were pulled out for the stabbings, as the screws on the flat at the time didn't like Andy; he had taken some of their fellow comrades hostage and slashed one of them some years earlier.

Andy had emergency surgery before being moved into intensive care. All in all, he lay in hospital for seven weeks before he returned to Shotts Prison. The Shotts screws put Andy in the segregation unit for some eighteen months before he was moved to Perth Prison. During his time there, he was involved in a major incident where a prisoner was found with his throat cut.

After that, Andy got moved to Glenochil and that is where I first met him. On first appearances, he didn't look like the madman that people were saying he was but, as you know, the truly dangerous ones never do look like your stereotypical movie hard men. Andy was rather fat around the middle, like quite a few of the other Scottish prison danger men. The bulk around their middle has, and there is no doubt in my mind, saved their lives when they have been involved in a knife fight.

Andy had only been in Glenochil for a matter of weeks

before the jail's first screw hostage took place. The morning before the hostage, Andy had been arguing with an old screw who used to work up at Peterhead when he had been there doing five years. The argument got out of hand, Andy left the office to get his knife, returned to the office and pulled the knife on the screw. When the screw saw what was happening, he lunged forward and grabbed Andy's arm. A struggle then ensued.

It was so funny; I witnessed this with my own eyes. Andy and the screw were like two WWF wrestlers. The others prisoners and I were locked behind the grille gates cheering Andy on when the chants, sung to the tune of 'Jingle Bells' started. It went like this: 'Stab a screw, stab a screw, stab a screw today, oh what fun it is to stab a screw on New Year's Day' – it was only 29 December.

Some five or six screws from another part of the prison came running into the hall. They all jumped on Andy and hit him with their riot batons before dragging him off down to the seg unit where he received a bad beating.

A couple of weeks after the screw hostage episode, Andy got his typewriter out. He used to remove the metal bar that held the little black wheel in place, go for his shower and sharpen the piece of steel on the concrete window frame. This took him some two or three months. He was planning on stabbing as many screws as he possibly could.

During this time, one of the boys that Andy had had a run-in with when he was in Shotts, Stevie Anderson (another lifer), was moved to the seg block in Glenochil. Andy set his plan in motion to stab him.

Andy and Stevie stood at their cell doors screaming at each other for some two weeks before Andy finally got his chance. The following just goes to show how cruel the screws are: when Stevie went for his shower, they didn't lock him in (prison protocol dictates that every prisoner should be locked into the shower).

After Stevie had been in the shower for some five minutes, they opened Andy up so that he could use the phone. When he was walking by the shower, he noticed that the door wasn't shut. He told the screw he had forgotten his phone book, ran back to his cell in the seg block, got his 7in piece of sharpened steel from under his mattress and ran along to the shower room, where he found Stevie standing naked with shampoo on his face.

Andy didn't need a second invitation: he stabbed Stevie six times. Stevie fell to the shower room floor, blood everywhere. Andy calmly walked out, flung the piece of steel down to the screws who had gathered at the bottom of the stairs and then, cool as you like, walked back along to his cell and shut his door.

The screws never even got their balls felt for leaving the shower door unlocked. They said that Andy had kicked it open, bursting the lock in the process. You see, the screws hated both of them, so they played them against each other until one of them came off worse than the other.

Stevie never forgot what the screws did to him. I will tell you later in this book, but I can say that he got them back big time for their little game in Glenochil seg block – a game that cost Stevie half of his liver. By now, Andy was looked upon as more than a hard bastard – he was seen as a madman. He was sent to the state hospital for some two years before he managed to get back to the mainstream prison system where, the last I heard, he has been doing OK. I wish you all the best, Andy. Hope things turn out good for you, pal.

2

Scottish Folklore Hard Bastards

I would like to take the time to highlight some of the older prisoners to have served some very long and very hard time up in Peterhead Prison from the 1950s to the early 1980s. Some of these convicts are legendary hard bastards in Scottish folklore.

Peterhead convict prison is on the very windy and wet northeast coastline of Scotland. What is so unique about this prison is that the convicts built the place themselves from a type of granite that only is found in the northeast of Scotland. Granite is one of the hardest stones to work with, and once it is set in cement it will last till the end of time.

Up until 1965, the prisoners who had the misfortune to spend time within its walls had to wear a ball and chain and a striped black-and-white, all-in-one overall jumpsuit with arrows all over the place. The convicts were taken from the prison on little trains some five miles away to the granite stone mines where they worked like slaves from 6.30am until 5.00pm, day in day out.

Come sunshine, rain or snow, these men were put

through their paces; the prison guards would stand above them with bolt-action rifles and cutlass swords. If you tried to escape from the mines, or from the prison in general, the guards could, and would, shoot you down.

When the convicts addressed a screw, they weren't allowed within a cutlass-sword length of him; if they overstepped the mark, the screw was well within his rights to run the sword clean through the prisoner. The guns and swords were still being used as late as the 1960s, as were the ball and chain. That is why – compared to the other prisons in Scotland – Peterhead convict prison is so unique. Here are some of the characters to have served time up there. Here are some of the tough characters to have served time up there.

OSCAR SLATER

Oscar Slater, a German Jew who had settled in Scotland, came under suspicion for the brutal murder and robbery of a wealthy old woman, Miss Marion Gilchrist (aged eighty-two) of 15 Queens Terrace, West Princess Street, in the West End of Glasgow, on 21 December 1908.

During their initial investigations, the police discovered that a valuable brooch was missing from the house. A few days later, someone reported that a man called Oscar Slater had been trying to sell a pawn ticket for a brooch. When the police investigated further, they discovered that Slater had taken the train to Liverpool on the night of the murder and, on 26 December, had sailed to New York on the SS *Lusitania*. His description fitted that of the murderer and the police arranged for him to be arrested when the ship docked in New York on 3 January 1909.

Two witnesses accompanied the police to New York and, when they were in the police station, both of them had Slater pointed out to them as he passed in a corridor. A few minutes later, both witnesses identified Slater as 'looking like' the man they had seen leaving the house where the woman had been killed.

Slater protested his innocence, but agreed to accompany the police back to Glasgow to stand trial for the murder. At the time of his arrest, Slater still had the pawn ticket on him. However, it was discovered that it was not a ticket for the stolen brooch, but for a brooch that Slater had owned for years and which he often pawned when he was short of money. They also discovered that the brooch had actually been pawned a few days before the murder had been committed. Slater also proved that his travel plans had been long standing and that many people knew he intended to leave Scotland for America. Nevertheless, the police insisted that Slater's hurried departure to Liverpool and his 'flight' on the *Lusitania*, along with the 'identification' by the two witnesses and evidence that he led a 'dissolute lifestyle' – drinking, gambling and 'living in sin' – indicated his guilt.

Against all the odds, Slater was charged with the murder and the fifteen-man jury found him guilty by a majority verdict of nine to six at the Edinburgh High Court on 6 May 1909. Lord Guthrie sentenced Oscar Slater to death. There was a huge public outcry against Slater's conviction and sentence and, on 26 May 1909, two days before he was due to be hanged, his death sentence was commuted to life imprisonment. Lucky Oscar.

Many academics, including Marshall Hall and the writer Edgar Wallace, were outraged at the injustice of Slater's trial and conviction and one man in particular, Sir Arthur Conan Doyle (creator of that great fictional detective, Sherlock Holmes), led a crusade to get justice for Slater.

Slater was incarcerated for nineteen years in the grim, granite prison of Peterhead, before continued pressure from the public led to an appeal being heard. His sentence was quashed on the grounds of misdirection in law and, in 1926, Slater was set free. He did not receive a pardon, but was awarded an ex-gratia payment of £6,000. He married in 1937 and, ironically, spent the Second World War as an internee, due to his Jewish-German origins. He died in America in 1948 and his conviction for the murder of Miss Gilchrist goes down as one of the most serious miscarriages of justice by the Scottish legal system.

ROBERT MEECHAN

I do not suppose that anyone can write a tale about any inhabitants of Scotland's prisons without mentioning the last man to be given the 'cat' in Scotland.

It happened in the late 1930s, when Robert Meechan was already in the punishment block after having assaulted a prison officer. Scottish prison governors have always been God-fearing and they even encouraged those in the cells to attend church and Bible classes. The bold Robert impressed and pleased the governor by requesting that he attend the Sunday Bible class and permission was readily given. But Robert had a more devious reason for attending Bible class.

Yearning for a smoke in the tobacco-barren punishment block, he decided that desperate measures were called for. Robert knew that the church organist smoked a pipe and, therefore, it followed that he would have a tobacco pouch somewhere on his person.

The Bible class was going strong; its large attendance was due more to the fact that it broke the tedium of prison nothingness than any desire to be nearer to God. The organist was in full tilt, belting out 'Onward Christian Soldiers', or something like it, when Robert rose to his feet and went forward to embrace him.

However, under cover of the 'embrace', Robert was actually doing a quick check of the petrified organist's pockets, searching for the elusive tobacco pouch. He succeeded in his mission and was clutching the tobacco pouch when he was tackled by the supervising screws and thrown to the floor.

Throughout the struggle, Robert held the pouch so tightly that it was impossible for the screws to get it from him. A compromise was finally reached: Robert was told that he could keep the tobacco if he gave back the pouch. This was agreed and a victorious Robert was left with his desired smoke. The organist got his pouch back and the governor compensated him for the stolen tobacco.

However, the terrified soldier of Christ never returned to the prison again.

Robert was sentenced to twenty lashes of the cat o' nine tails for the Bible-class escapade, all of which were delivered on a triangular frame in the prison bathhouse – the brass mountings for the frame can still be seen there to this day. When he was untied from the frame after the beating, the hard bastard performed a back flip and declared 'Give me a couple of fags and I'll take the same again'!

He must have really meant it too, because, three years later in Parkhurst Prison, he assaulted a prison officer and was sentenced to the cat once again.

JOHNNY RAMENSKY

Johnny Ramensky was the first person ever to escape and get away from Peterhead Prison successfully. Of all the cracksmen (safebreakers) who came out of Scotland, there is no doubt that Johnny Ramensky stood head and shoulders above his closest contemporaries. Born in Glenboig, Lanarkshire, in 1905 of Lithuanian parents, Johnny had an austere childhood, after his mother was left to bring up the family on her own following her husband's death in a mining accident.

After leaving school at fourteen, Johnny followed in his father's footsteps and went down the mines. However, by the age of sixteen, many of the mines were starting to lay off their men and Johnny joined the ranks of the unemployed.

Unable to stand the cards-and-dominoes life of the

passive unemployed, Johnny decided that his experience as an apprentice shot-blaster would stand him in good stead as a safe-blower, and that is what he became.

His safe-blowing career began in the early twenties when Johnny specialised in blowing safes in garages and small factories. He was eventually captured on the roof of a factory and was sentenced to borstal. From then on, through most of his twenties, he was in and out of prison.

He escaped from Peterhead Prison in 1934, but was captured crossing the road bridge at Ellon where the police routinely set up a roadblock whenever an escape occurred. Taken back to Peterhead, he was promptly thrown into the punishment block where he was shackled hand and foot. News of this treatment caused a public outcry and the authorities were forced to abandon the barbaric practice. It left Johnny with the dubious honour of being the last man to have been shackled in Scotland.

In 1939, Johnny was sentenced to five years in Peterhead and, in 1942, two months before his sentence was due to finish, he was approached by a War Office official. Johnny was taken to London, where he was asked by the War Department to work behind enemy lines. Johnny agreed to this, but had to return to Peterhead to complete his sentence before he could take up this work.

After his release from prison, Johnny was given a specialist course of commando training, taught all about the latest explosives and was allowed to practise on new safes. Once he had completed his training, Johnny was parachuted behind enemy lines with orders to blow safes and to steal military plans. He carried out many successful missions for the British Army.

During the invasion of Italy, Johnny blew open fourteen safes in one day in the headquarters of the German Army. Perhaps his greatest coup, however, came when he blew open Reichmarschall Goering's safe in his house at Karinhall.

One story goes that Johnny was awarded the DCM (Distinguished Conduct Medal); another claimed that it was the Military Medal. Whatever it was, Johnny Ramensky certainly deserved it!

Once he was demobbed, Johnny found it difficult to adjust to normal life and soon resumed his criminal ways. He was caught in the act of blowing a safe in the north of England and, because of his Army record, received a lenient five-year sentence.

In 1952, Johnny escaped from Peterhead again. This time his escape became big news and the sympathetic newspaper reporting built him into a folk hero. However, once again, Johnny was recaptured at the same bridge, and by the same police officer, too! On his return to Peterhead, Johnny was swamped by letters from well-wishers.

After his release in 1955, Johnny decided to turn his hand to some literary effort, but fell foul of the Official Secrets Act, which forbade him from exposing any details about his military career. Thwarted in his literary ambition, Johnny reverted to his 'tools' once again. In the summer of 1955, he blew open the strongroom and two safes inside a bank, where he stole £8,000 and the contents of several strong boxes.

In late 1955, Johnny was captured raiding a bank in Rutherglen, near Glasgow, and a severe judge, Lord Carmont (the man who had smashed the Glasgow Razor gangs in the 1950s by handing out double-figure sentences), sentenced him to a harsh ten-year term.

Once again Peterhead played host to its famous prisoner. While serving this sentence, another well known Glasgow figure, Darky Davidson, who worked in the sick bay of the jail, helped Johnny with an escape plan. Using his privileged position, Darky lifted floorboards in the doctor's office and hid Johnny in the space underneath.

The idea was for Johnny to stay hidden until the roadblocks were lifted and he could then get clear. Darky kept Johnny supplied with food and drink, but impatience got the better of Johnny and he tried to escape too soon. His face was so well known that passengers on a bus spotted him walking along the road and reported the sighting to the police.

Johnny was recaptured within hours and returned to Peterhead. His status as a folk hero rose to such an extent that two folk songs were penned in his honour: 'Set Ramensky Free' was recorded and sung by the Scottish folk singer Roddy McMillan, while even Norman Buchan, a Member of Parliament, got into the spirit of things with 'The Ballad of Johnny Ramensky'.

Released from prison in 1964, it wasn't too long before Johnny was facing a High Court judge, for being caught on the roof of a Woolworths store in Paisley. This time, a more sympathetic judge let him off with two years.

In 1967, the irrepressible Johnny tackled another bank in Rutherglen, but by now the safes were getting better and Johnny's skills were on the wane. He packed so much gelignite into the space behind the keyhole that the blast blew out nearby windows. The safe was empty, though, and Johnny was captured as he tried to flee the scene. Outside in the street, he was brought to the ground by a young constable, who started punching Johnny about the head. In self-defence, Johnny struck out at the policeman and, as a result, the charge of police assault was added to that of attempted robbery.

Johnny pleaded guilty to the safe-blowing charge, but indignantly defended himself on the assault charge. Known to everyone as 'Gentle Johnny', he was more upset about being charged with assault than the safe-blowing offence and he was delighted when the jury returned a not guilty verdict on the assault charge; he happily accepted a four-year stretch for the safe-blowing. The irony was that although the safe had been empty, Johnny missed a sum of £80,000 that had been placed in an unlocked drawer nearby.

Now getting old, Johnny found his acrobatic feats of climbing more difficult to accomplish and, in 1970, he fell from a roof and spent fourteen weeks in hospital recovering from his injuries. He left the hospital to begin a two-year sentence.

Upon his release from prison after serving the two years, the mad bastard was once again caught on a roof at midnight, but as he had not actually broken into the premises, he got away with a one-year sentence for attempted burglary.

This last sentence proved too much for Johnny and he collapsed in Perth Prison. He was taken to Perth hospital, but died within a few weeks in 1972.

Johnny Ramensky's funeral in the Gorbals was attended by hundreds of mourners, all of whom came to show their respects for a brave, if misguided, man.

ARTHUR THOMPSON

Arthur Thompson was born in the Provanmill district of Glasgow, the third eldest in a family of four brothers. The first year or so of his life was spent living in a tenement building, before the family were rehoused in the slum clearance district of Blackhill, where Arthur then stayed for most of his life.

Managing to avoid the pitfalls of approved school and borstal as a youth, Arthur grew into manhood with a growing reputation as a fighter. It was this reputation, and his confidence in his own strength and abilities, which made Arthur decide that the quickest route to riches was to take over from the reigning gangsters of that time.

In 1955, he tried his hand at bank robbery, attempting to blow open the vault of a bank in Beauly, Invernesshire, along with his safecracker pal, Paddy Meehan. They were both captured and Paddy, because of a long list of previous convictions, was sentenced to six years. Arthur, whose record was comparatively mild, got three. In his entire career, Arthur only served four prison sentences, the longest of them being four years for 'reset' (receiving stolen goods). However, the failure of the bank robbery taught him a salutary lesson and, when he was released, he decided to turn his proven talent for violence to profit from protection rackets. He did this by making a frontal attack on the two top men of the day in Glasgow.

Although he always denied it, Arthur was 'credited' with the shooting of Glasgow gangster Teddy Martin and the beating up of the feared Algie Earns in the city centre. Both of these men ran protection rackets in pubs, clubs and street bookies and now, following their demise, Arthur was 'The Man'. He was never charged with either of these two incidents, but anyone 'in the know' was aware that Arthur Thompson had made a decisive leap onto the criminal ladder. Unopposed, Arthur took over the protection rackets and moved into the drinking club scene, opening The Raven Club and becoming a part-owner of the Hanover Club in the city centre. It was from these two places that he ruled his growing empire.

These two clubs were very successful, but the police viewed them as criminal hangouts and strove to close them down. After a particularly serious assault, where a man had been slashed repeatedly about the face, the police used fire-safety rules to keep the doors of both clubs shut. Arthur was charged with assault and appeared at the High Court, only for the case to be dropped through a lack of witnesses.

After the closure of his clubs, Arthur opened up an

illegal street bookmaking business. He did this quite openly, yet the police decided not to arrest him for it. A senior policeman said that Arthur actually *wanted* a conviction for running a bookmaking business, as this would explain away any large amounts of money he might be found with in the future.

Of course, Arthur had his rivals and he conducted a running feud with the Welsh family, also from Blackhill, for years. This feud finally came to a head in 1966 when Arthur rammed a van off the road, embedding it in a lamppost and killing its two occupants, Patrick Welsh and James Goldie. Arthur was charged with the double murder and was tried at the High Court: he was found not guilty yet again. Three months after the van 'accident', a bomb meant for Arthur went off under his car, missing him but killing his mother-in-law. Later, the two Welsh brothers, Martin and Henry, were acquitted at the High Court of murder and the bombing of Arthur's car.

In fact there were three serious attempts on Arthur's life. The first one was the car bomb, which had such tragic results. A few years later, an 'unknown' assailant shot him in the groin, but he had the bullet removed and claimed that he had injured himself with a broken drill-bit. The third attempt came later in his life, when a young man, a friend of his son, ran him over with a car.

By 1972, Arthur owned two public houses in Glasgow: the first, The Provanmill Inn, being the premier pub in his own Blackhill area. The second pub, The Right Half in George Street, was close to the city centre. Success followed success and Arthur was reputed to have a finger in most of the criminal activity in the city. He moved into the demolition and the scrap-metal trade and was doing extremely well in legitimate business.

Of course, like most serious criminals in the late 1970s and early '80s, Arthur found himself drawn irresistibly into the burgeoning drug trade. It was his son, Arthur Jr, who took the lead in the drug business, unashamedly capitalising on his father's reputation and wealth to do so. But although the profits were huge, it was their involvement in the drugs business that was to bring heartache to the Thompson family.

In 1991, young Arthur, who was on his first home leave from prison after serving six years of an eleven-year sentence for drug dealing, was shot and killed outside his own house in Provanmill Road. Arthur Jr had been vociferous in announcing that he would soon be out for good and that he would take over the drugs business. But others had moved on during Arthur's long absence and although all of them were old pals, there was no love lost between drug dealers.

Four men were said to have been involved in the 'execution' of Arthur Jr. What is known is that on the day of Arthur Jr's funeral, two of them were found shot dead in the back of a car outside their local pub. To this day, no one has ever been charged with their slaying.

Paul Ferris, once the best friend of young Arthur, was later charged with his shooting but, after the longest murder trial in Scottish history, he was found not guilty.

Some eighteen months later, in 1993, Arthur Sr, a man

who had survived a bomb, a bullet and a charging car, died peacefully in his sleep from a heart attack. A legend was dead.

PADDY MEEHAN

In 1933, Paddy Meehan, born in the Gorbals district of Glasgow, earned his first conviction for stealing old timber from a derelict building. Later that same year, he was caught pulling a branch from a tree and once again appeared before the sheriff on a charge of malicious damage. In 1934, when he was nine years old, young Paddy was caught riding a stolen bicycle and was charged with theft. Because this was his third conviction, he was promptly sentenced to two years in an approved school and, for the next nine years, he was in and out of one approved school after another. In 1944, at the age of seventeen, he was charged with breaking and entering a garage and stealing tools. He was sentenced to ten months' borstal training.

In 1945, shortly after he had been released from borstal, Paddy got married, but within a short space of time he was indicted for breaking into a shop and stealing clothing coupons. This time he was sentenced to fifteen months' imprisonment in Barlinnie.

Paddy blew his first safe in 1947 – once again to obtain clothing coupons – and from then on this became his favoured method of 'earning'. He had a successful run of just over a year before he was captured. Then, in 1948, he was sentenced to three years for safe-blowing again and was sent to Peterhead Prison.

When he was released, in 1950, Paddy kept a low profile and worked at his 'trade' with some degree of success until 1953, when he was caught breaking into an explosives store. This resulted in a two-year sentence and once again Paddy found himself in Peterhead.

When he was released from this sentence, Paddy returned to Peterhead and helped another prisoner, Teddy Martin of Glasgow, to escape. Once Martin was clear of the prison, Paddy took him to a rented house in the town where they laid low. It was well known that Peterhead's isolation made it easy for the police to put up roadblocks and this was how most escapees, Johnny Ramensky in particular, were recaptured. With this in mind, Teddy's friends had already prepared a set of prisoner's clothing and, after a phone call to report that Teddy was out, this clothing was placed in an empty house in Glasgow.

After an appropriate delay, the Glasgow police received an anonymous phone call telling them that Teddy was hiding out at a certain address, but when they raided the house, all they found was the prisoner's clothing. Satisfied that Teddy Martin had reached the city, the police lifted the roadblocks, thus leaving the way clear for Paddy to drive Teddy home in style.

In 1955, Paddy blew open the safe in a bank in Oban and stole £12,000 in cash as well as a large amount of jewellery from safety-deposit boxes. However, he was captured later that same year attempting to blow open the safe in a bank in Beauly, in the Highlands. He was sentenced to six years for his troubles.

During this sentence, a group of prisoners piled onto a

lorry that was unloading next to the football pitch and, in a desperate bid for freedom, smashed through a gate out onto the road. Unfortunately, the lorry went straight across the road and crashed into a ditch. Paddy leapt from the lorry and ran to the prison gate shouting that he had been kidnapped and demanding to be let in. He got away with it, too!

After completing his six-year sentence, Paddy went to London and in 1961 he was caught once again blowing open a safe in a branch of the Co-op. This time he was sent to the Old Bailey and given eight years' preventative detention. It was while he was serving this sentence that he escaped from Nottingham Prison and apparently disappeared.

What Paddy had done, and he told this to Scottish record-breaking robber James Crosbie when they shared time together in the Peterhead punishment block, was to travel to West Germany and on to the East German border. When he was there, he demanded asylum!

The East Germans allowed him into the country, but put him into a soft prison that was mainly used for holding people such as journalists and political prisoners. The East German officials did not really believe that he had escaped from prison in England or, for that matter, that he actually wanted asylum in East Germany when every second person there was trying to escape. They suspected that Paddy might have some other reason for appearing among them.

He was held in the prison for seventeen months before they finally decided that he was telling the truth. What finally convinced his interrogator was the fact that Paddy, more often than not, refused to go on exercise if the weather wasn't nice. The other prisoners in the place, all first-timers, were always tearing at their doors when the guard shouted '*Frei Stunde*!' (free hour), while Paddy would just lie in his bed and ask what the weather was like. Only an old con, the interrogator thought, would behave like that.

So, finally, Paddy was offered asylum and a job to go with it. It so happened that he was fluent in German (this was what had made him decide to head to the country in the first place), so he was offered a job in the town library transcribing books. However, he was warned him that if he got into any trouble in East Germany he would go to a real prison for a very long time... and East German prisons were much tougher than their counterparts in the UK. Paddy was given a choice: stay in the Eastern sector or go home. He chose to go home and so they dropped him off at Checkpoint Charlie and into the arms of the British security services; they flew him back to England.

On his return, Paddy demanded that his seventeen months in the East German prison should count as part of his eight-year sentence. He even claimed that he had saved the prison department money by letting the East Germans pay for his keep! They fell for that one, too!

Paddy was initially sent to Wandsworth Prison but, within a few months, he was transferred to Blundeston in Suffolk. It was while he was there that he met James Griffiths, the man who was to play such a catastrophic part in his life. Later on, Paddy was transferred to

Parkhurst and was released from there in 1968, heading straight back to Glasgow.

Later on in 1968, James Griffiths, the man he had met in Blundeston, turned up at his house and they began associating together. Griffiths at this time was stealing luxury cars and those he couldn't sell he would push off a cliff into the deep waters of Loch Awe in Argyleshire. It was Paddy who suggested that they break into the Motor Taxation Office in the town of Stranraer where they could steal unused logbooks, which would enable them to sell the stolen cars more easily.

They set off one evening to drive to Stranraer, their route taking them through the seaside town of Ayr. However, once they reached Stranraer, Paddy, for one reason or another, decided not to carry on with the break-in and they returned to Glasgow, once again passing through the town of Ayr.

What they did not know was that, on the same night, two Glasgow criminals were also in Ayr, intent on carrying out a 'tie-up' robbery at the bungalow home of a Mr and Mrs Ross. Mr Ross was the proprietor of a Glasgow bingo hall and it was rumoured among the Glasgow criminals that he kept his money at home.

Late that night, the two robbers forced their way into the bungalow and attacked the elderly couple, beating both of them up until Mr Ross told them where he kept his money. After giving them the required information, the couple were tied up and forced into a small cupboard and left there while the villains helped themselves. After getting the money, both robbers then settled down to wait until morning, when it would be safer to for one of them to go and pick up their car.

At 6.00am the following morning, one of the men began to walk towards the centre of town where the car had been inconspicuously parked. Not far from the bungalow, two police officers stopped him to ask why he was in the area. He told a cock-and-bull story about being drunk and staying at a friend's house overnight and that he was catching the early bus to Glasgow.

His explanation satisfied the police and they directed him to the bus depot and let him carry on. The man returned to the bungalow with the car to pick up his accomplice and they drove away, having told Mr Ross that they would telephone the police when they were clear. They failed to keep this promise and, by the time the elderly pair were discovered, Mrs Ross was already dead and her husband was in a serious condition.

The police investigation team soon discovered that Paddy Meehan had been in the area that night and he was brought in for questioning. Under the circumstances, Paddy felt that he had no option but to explain why he had been in Ayr that night. He told the police that he had passed through because he had gone to Stranraer to break into the Motor Taxation Office and gave up Griffiths' name to support his alibi.

However, when the police went to interview Griffiths, he fired a shotgun at them and then began to shoot indiscriminately at passers-by in the street with a high-powered rifle. He shot and wounded seven people as armed police raced to surround the building.

Griffiths managed to escape from the building and hijacked a car at gunpoint, but the car crashed at the Round Toll, on the corner of Possil Road. He raced from the car into a pub, brandishing his rifle and demanding a bottle of brandy.

An old newspaper vendor, Willie Hughes, went to pick up his glass and Griffiths shot him dead. On leaving the pub, Griffiths hijacked a lorry and ordered the driver to head away from the scene. A police sergeant spotted the hijack and followed the lorry in a taxi to Springburn, about two miles away. Once in Springburn, the lorry turned into Kay Street, a short cul-de-sac, forcing Griffiths to abandon it and race into a tenement building.

He took refuge in an empty flat and began shooting at people from the window. The police soon had the building surrounded but, by this time, Griffiths had shot several more innocent passers-by. Finally, Chief Superintendent Callum Finlay shot Griffiths through the letterbox of the flat, killing him instantly.

On the day he died, in 1972, Griffiths had shot a total of fourteen innocent people before he was himself killed by gunfire. Many people believe that Griffiths died in exactly the fashion he wanted.

With Griffiths now dead in spectacular style, Paddy had no one to support his story and he was promptly charged with the murder of Mrs Ross, the assault on Mr Ross and the robbery of their house. One of the main pieces of evidence against him was that Mr Ross stated that the two robbers had called each other Pat and Jim when they addressed one another. However, he also said that both men had strong Glaswegian accents; something that Griffiths did not possess as he was from Rochdale in Lancashire.

In January 1970, Paddy stood trial at the High Court in Glasgow and was found guilty of the robbery and the murder of Rachel Ross. He was sentenced to life imprisonment and sent to Peterhead, loudly protesting his innocence.

By this stage, it was already well known to everyone in the Glasgow criminal world that Paddy was indeed innocent. His defence team, Nicholas Fairbairn QC, his solicitor Joe Beltrami and his MP Mr McElhone were also convinced of his innocence and fought continuously to have the case reopened, only to see their petitions to the Secretary of State for Scotland routinely dismissed. Writer Ludovic Kennedy joined the campaign and also fought for his release. He even wrote a book, *Presumption of Innocence*, to support Paddy's case.

As a protest against his conviction, Paddy elected to serve his time in solitary confinement in the punishment block at Peterhead and, for the next six years, he fought to have his case reopened. He now claimed that the British secret service had set him up because he had information regarding the escape from Wormwood Scrubs of George Blake, the Russian master spy.

During his time in East Germany, Paddy claimed, he had been taken to Moscow and interrogated by the Russians regarding all aspects of prison security in England. He also said that they had made specific enquiries regarding George Blake and the chances of getting him out of the Scrubs (prison). He claimed that he had reported all of this to MI5 and had warned them that the Russians intended to break Blake out of the jail.

Paddy's wild claims were dismissed and, although he continued to blame MI5 for setting him up to get both him and his knowledge out of the way, no credence was ever given to his tale.

It was found out that, a few days after the murder, a well known Glasgow petty criminal, Ian Waddle, had approached a solicitor, Mr Carlin, and paid him the sum of £200 as a retainer: 'In case I am questioned over the Ayr murder.' At this stage, another MP, Mr William Ross, called for an urgent review of the case. Again, this demand was refused. Later, during a trial at the High Court, Waddell was asked about paying Carlin the £200. He denied that this had ever happened. Mr Carlin, however, said that it had indeed been true and Waddell was charged with perjury and sentenced to three years' imprisonment.

In Peterhead, Paddy himself, reading law books, discovered an old statute that should have enabled him to get the case reopened. It was called 'A Bill of Criminal Letters' and would enable him to take the police to court to be re-examined on their evidence. However, this was also rejected.

In 1973, following his release from his three-year sentence for perjury, Waddell announced that he wanted to confess and told a newspaper – who taped the interview – that he had committed the murder. However, the Scottish *Daily Mail* did not carry the front-page confession until 1975. At about the same time, the BBC's *Panorama* programme broadcast an interview with Waddell, where he once again admitted to the murder.

Still the authorities did nothing either to reopen the case or to investigate Waddell's claims. Meanwhile, a well-known, extremely violent, Glasgow criminal, William 'Tank' McGuiness, had already told solicitor Beltrami that he had committed the murder and that Paddy was innocent.

However, because of the strict rules of client confidentiality, Beltrami was unable to report McGuiness' confession. Then, in 1976, Tank McGuiness was found dead and Mr Beltrami, no longer bound under the rules of confidentiality, was able to reveal his confession. When the details of the confession were made public, the Ayrshire police checked back to 1966 and found the report regarding the man that had been stopped and questioned by a patrol that night. This and other details proved the validity of McGuiness' confession.

As a direct result of Beltrami's revelations, the Secretary of State, Bruce Millan, announced in the House of Commons that, due to new evidence in the Meehan case, he would now recommend that the Queen grant Patrick Connolly Meehan a Royal Pardon.

Paddy spent more than six years in solitary confinement until he was pardoned for a crime he had not committed and, for this, he was initially awarded the paltry sum of £7,500 as compensation. This caused a public outcry and questions were asked in the House of

Commons about the fairness of the award. One of the reasons put forward by the official who arrived at the £7,500 sum was that, because Paddy had been a criminal for almost his entire life, it was more than likely that he would have been in prison anyway for most of the six years. In fact it was not until 1984 that Paddy finally received a settlement of £47,915 in compensation for his wrongful conviction for murder.

When he left prison, Paddy decided that he had had enough of crime and imprisonment. He moved back in with his wife and became a successful door-to-door salesman for a double-glazing company. He never returned to crime and, on 14 August 1994, sadly lost his battle with throat cancer.

Paddy was, quite justifiably, never happy with the wording of the Royal Pardon. He always said that it should have been an apology, admitting that a grave mistake had been made instead of a 'pardon' for a crime that he had not committed in the first place. One of his books, *Innocent Villain* (Macmillan, 1978), is still available in bookshops; his other, *Framed by MI5*, is now out of print.

WALTER SCOTT ELLIS

Walter Scott Ellis, otherwise known as the arch criminal 'Watty', was part of the infamous Hole in the Wall gang that was responsible for a string of armed robberies. However, what made Watty infamous was that he was the second to last man in Scotland to miss the hangman's rope: he had been looking at a death sentence until he was found not guilty of the murder he had initially been sentenced for.

There is a procedure in the Scottish prison system whereby any prisoner can write directly to the Scottish Home Secretary – at least that is what you are led to believe – with any complaint, request or observation that you might have. All you have to do is put in a governor's request for a petition form and one will be handed to you almost immediately. You then write out your 'petition', seal it in the envelope provided (you don't even need a stamp), hand it in at the Prison Officer's desk and off it goes to the Home Department offices in Edinburgh.

There is none of the frustrating business of having to explain anything to an educationally challenged screw or of being obliged to seek advice from your 'personal officer'. If you want a petition form you get a petition form: it is one of the very few rights Scottish prisoners have. Subject to not using bad language, you can write about whatever you like in your petition. It really is all very civilised.

Approximately six weeks after despatching your petition, the governor will call you up and will read you the reply to your petition. You will also be given a written copy of the Home Secretary's reply. It seems to be a very satisfactory procedure all round.

Needless to say, Peterhead's prisoner population has generated a constant stream of these petitions and some of the guys became very clever at penning them. One of the most prolific writers of such petitions was Walter Scott Ellis, who, in around 1968, was sentenced to twenty-one years for an armed bank robbery in which the manager was shot, and another charge of attempted murder after he hit someone on the head with an axe. Walter was not so much a hard man, being of slight build and not the least bit threatening looking, as simply a cold and vicious bastard. Throughout his sentence he would not conform to normal prison behaviour, refusing to come out of his cell for association (they call it 'recreation' in English prisons, which only goes to show that the Scottish use of the English language is more accurate).

Walter was still on the 'A' list when he was ten years into his sentence. It was a certain screw who handled 'A' men that prompted Walter to write this particular petition, which I thank James Crosbie for recalling:

To: *The Right Honourable Secretary of State for Scotland*:
Dear Sir,
I would like to complain about the constant strip searches I have to suffer in here. Most of the time they are pretty normal and do not give me any cause for concern. However, there is one particular turnkey [Walter insisted in addressing all screws as turnkeys] who is disturbing me with his zeal when carrying out these searches. At least once a week, this turnkey insists on coming to my cell and giving me a strip search. Now I know he is allowed to do this and I am not complaining about his seemingly insatiable desire to see me in the nude, but this turnkey always makes me strip

down to my vest and then gets me to pirouette about my cell like a demented ballerina, so that he can freely inspect my bare buttocks and my other dangly bits.

It is obvious to me that this turnkey is a pervert; I can tell by the way his eyes pop open and because of the fact that his breathing sounds funny. However, if he gets his kicks out of watching me spinning around and my private parts merrily jiggling up and down, that is up to him. In fact I am not complaining about his perversion. What I am complaining about is *that I am beginning to get to like it*!

Yours sincerely,
Walter Scott Ellis

WILLIAM 'POKEY' TURNER

Every petition receives a reply, and I am in no doubt that many of my readers are curious to know what sort of reply Walter received. However, before telling you that, I will describe the petition process in a little more detail.

The petition process in Scotland is a well-established complaints routine, although, as I have already mentioned, a prisoner can petition for any reason. When a prisoner has something to complain about, he asks for a petition form. These blue forms are pre-addressed to The Right Honourable Secretary of State for Scotland, so there is no doubt in the prisoner's mind that his petition is being handled at the highest levels.

It usually takes about six weeks from the time the petition is submitted for a reply to surface in the governor's office. When this happens, the writer of the petition is BU'd (brought up) before the governor, much like a disciplinary hearing. The con is marched into the orderly room and, once there, he gives the governor his name, number and sentence and says 'Sir' at the end. Having thus established that this is indeed the felon who penned the petition, his High Heid Yin (High Head One) opens an official brown envelope and proceeds to read out the Secretary of State for Scotland's carefully considered reply. Unfortunately for most cons (about ninety-nine per cent in actual fact) – and in Walter's case – this is this is where the petition charade breaks down. In ninety-nine per cent of cases, the governor will study the reply, as though it does contain a 'carefully considered' reply, will purse his lips and nod to himself, obviously in full agreement with the Secretary of State, and will then say, as in the case of Walter's petition regarding the perverted screw: 'Ellis, the Secretary of State has carefully considered the matters arising from your petition and I am instructed to inform you of his reply.'

There is a long, pregnant pause, before the carefully considered words are officially read out to the petitioner.

'Please inform the prisoner that he has no grounds for complaint.'

And that's that.

'About turn, quick march. Next!'

However, there was one persistent bastard, William

'Pokey' Turner, of the battered, baldy-head, squashed-nose, slashed-face and cauliflower-ear brigade, who tried to outwit the system. On one occasion, he was shuffling out of the governor's office after having been given the answer to yet another of his many petitions. And yes, once again the reply was: 'Please inform the prisoner that he has no grounds for complaint.'

'What was your answer?'

The inevitable question was put to the darkly muttering Pokey as he shuffled out onto the bottom flat of A-Hall.

'Fucking load o' shite!' Pokey uttered to no one in particular and everyone in general. 'Same every fucking time, so it is! No fucking grounds for complaint.'

'Well whit dae ye' keep writing them for?' someone interrupted Pokey's manic muttering, 'Ye' know ye' always get the same answer.'

'Oh aye, dae ah?' Pokey turned his bleary eyes on his critic, 'I'll tell ye' whit...' His face screwed up into a crafty expression: 'I bet I fuck them wi' ma next wan!'

'Oh aye,' the cynic's voice boomed out. 'Whit's it going tae be aboot this time?'

'Jist you wait and see,' Pokey mumbled mysteriously. 'I'll definitely fuck'em this time. Jist you wait and see if ah don't,' he muttered on, his bottom lip thrust out like a wet roller towel as he contemplated his next fiendish move.

A few days later, Pokey requested a petition form and off he went to write his latest diatribe against the system that continuously treated him in such an off-handed, cavalier fashion. This time, though, Pokey really intended to baffle 'them at head office'.

Locked up in the safety of his cell, our Pokey penned a petition along similar lines to the following:

To: *The Right Honourable Secretary of State for Scotland*:

Dear Sir,

U wiyks kuje ti cunolub abiyt the sutatuib ub the orudi grtr as Pryrthrsf. Rbrty yimz z etlyrs Oryuyuib ygr dsmr abssert... viykf kity okrsrtd yrt sbf tuvr nr s otiort troky di I vsn dndoe yhsy ysnsrt id svbtusslly domrnr sy grsd iggubr hgat bsd yrkk nr dinr ig yhr hoof nred.

U sn grf lyo euyth skests hryyubg yr same anser and U fp biy kukr iy' Ygsbj git ostubh di bycg syyrbyiub yi nr.

Your sincerely,
William Turner.

'There,' said Pokey, sticking down the envelope – another device to let you think that the petition is confidential between you and The Right Honourable – ha, ha, ha. 'There, that'll sort the bastards out. See what kind of answer they give me for that!'

Pokey's crafty stratagem had to be applauded and he waited anxiously for the six-week period to pass. Then, one day, Pokey got BU'd. The answer had arrived at last!

'Name, number and sentence to the governor, and say Sir!' the old chief barked as Pokey, grinning all over his face, marched into the office.

The governor opened the envelope and prepared to read out the carefully considered reply. He studied it for a few minutes, shaking his head, and finally passed the answer to the waiting Pokey.

'Here, Turner,' he said. 'You'd better read this for yourself.'

Pokey stared at the paper for a full ten seconds before bellowing out: 'Whit the fuck's this? Ah canny read this shite!'

The governor took the paper back and looked at the writing again. It read something along the lines of: 'Ijesae yvfrjrb tge irysuber tgat gr gsa bi griyhbfd git vinijdubt.'

'Well it is quite plain to me, Turner,' the governor told the gaping Pokey. 'The answer quite clearly states: "Please inform the prisoner that he has no grounds for complaint." About turn, quick march! Next!'

Pokey's baffled expression told its own tale to the waiting prisoners. Fucked again! The lesson here is clear: you will never beat the system.

JAMES 'JIMMY' BOYLE

Jimmy Boyle needs no introduction: he has done it all from a two-bob ned all the way to becoming Scotland's most dangerous prisoner. After his life sentence, he went on to become a multimillionaire author and a world-famous sculptor. Barlinnie's infamous special unit was opened especially for him and a select band of others. There are a few books and even a film out about this man's life of crime and his struggles against the system.

Jimmy is yet another product of the Gorbals area of Glasgow, and was the second youngest in a family of four brothers. With his mother doing three different cleaning jobs in order to support her family, the young Boyle spent much of his time dodging school and roaming the tenement streets and backcourts along with other kids who were in much the same family situation.

Stealing and running about in a gang had always been the norm for children born into the ghetto of the Gorbals and Jimmy was no exception. He was admired by his peers for his derring-do activities, but it was when he turned twelve and graduated to Saint Bonaventure's Junior Secondary school that he moved up a league and began to build a reputation for himself as a good fighter, as well as an accomplished shop-lifter and thief.

By now he had become the leader of 'The Scull' gang, a breakaway group from the 'Young Wild Cumbie'. However, despite his involvement in stealing and shop breaking, it was not until 1957, at the age of thirteen, that Jimmy recorded his first criminal conviction. He was charged with theft after stealing the money and contents of a bubble-gum machine.

Jimmy was held in Larchgrove Remand Home before being sentenced to two years' probation. That same year, he received a sentence of fourteen days for breaking and entering office premises. In 1958, it was shop breaking and this time his sentence was twenty-eight days – his 'record' was growing.

Jimmy left school at the age of fifteen and, later that year, 1959, he was arrested for stealing a safe from a garage. However, the police could find no evidence to lead to a conviction. Later that same year, however, he was caught stealing a cash-box from a fairground stall and was once again charged with theft. When he appeared in front of the sheriff, he was remanded for reports before being sentenced to an indefinite period of training at Saint John's, an approved school that stood next door to the by-now-familiar Larchgrove Remand Home in the east of Glasgow. Jimmy failed to return from a home leave, preferring the lure of London to the discipline of an approved school.

One night in London, Jimmy and a pal came across an electrical-goods shop. Its window had been broken, so they reached in to help themselves to two transistor radios. As soon as they had their hands on the loot, two constables leapt out from their hiding place and arrested them. After a court appearance, Jimmy was ordered to return to Saint John's, from where he was released in 1960.

Jimmy had several jobs during the 1960s, including a spell in the shipyards. He decided to try London once again, often travelling back to Glasgow for a quick visit. In 1961, during one of these flying visits, he was arrested for breaking into a shop and was remanded to Barlinnie Prison for borstal reports.

Later, he was sentenced to borstal training and transferred to Polmont borstal. His time in Polmont was uneventful, except that he was found to be suffering from bronchial tuberculosis and had to undergo two operations in hospital. He was released from Polmont in 1962, after serving just fourteen months of his sentence.

In 1962, Jimmy became involved in his first violent

crime when he was caught up in a running gang fight in Crown Street, Glasgow. Several innocent passers-by were stabbed during the mêlée and Jimmy ended up being charged with seven accounts of serious assault. Once again he was remanded to Bar-L but, in January 1963, he was bailed out on the assault cases.

Shortly after this, Jimmy was set upon by a rival gang of brothers, who hacked at him with hatchets and other weapons, leaving him for dead in the street. However, he managed to make his way to hospital and received treatment. The next day, his enemies were saying they had 'done Boyle up' and that he was 'finished'.

In order to scotch the rumours, Jimmy, with the help of his friends, dressed himself smartly and went down to the pub where the brothers were drinking and boasting of how they had 'tuned Boyle up good style'. The brothers were stunned when their 'victim' appeared at the bar in apparent good health, nodding and grinning over at them, totally demolishing their morale and laying the lie of their boasts.

In 1963, Jimmy went back down to London and began money lending. However, one evening, a policeman stopped him for questioning and Jimmy assaulted him. He was sentenced to six weeks in 'The Scrubs' and was 'gate arrested' by the Glasgow police on the morning of his release. Flown under escort to Glasgow, he was put on trial for the seven assault charges he was already on bail for and was sentenced to two years.

Back in Barlinnie, he was suspected of stabbing another prisoner, but wasn't charged due to a lack of evidence. However, not to be outdone, the authorities placed him on Rule 36 – a fancy name for solitary confinement – saying that he was a subversive element. After six months of Rule 36, Jimmy was allowed back into the mainstream population in A-Hall, an adult wing, where it was hoped that the older men would have a calming influence on him. He completed his sentence without any serious trouble.

By now Jimmy's gang had moved into the protection game, looking after the moneylenders as well as illegal Shebeen (unlicensed drink sellers) operators. Money was pouring in and all the gang had to do was to make sure that everybody behaved themselves. Jimmy settled down a little, sharing his life with his new girlfriend, Margaret.

One night, eight detectives raided Jimmy's flat and arrested him on a murder charge. To his surprise, Jimmy found himself accused of murdering and robbing a man called Lynch; the murder part of the charge made it a capital crime and one where the death penalty could be imposed. He was sent for trial at the High Court in Glasgow. However, owing to Jimmy's stout denials of even knowing the murdered man, a good alibi and a dearth of witnesses for the prosecution, the trial ended on the second day with Jimmy walking free from the courtroom.

Two weeks after his acquittal, Jimmy became involved in a fight with two men, with one of them losing an eye and with the other receiving a severe cut to his hand. The police then discovered that Jimmy had been at a party at which a man had been stabbed to death and he promptly found himself on remand in the Bar-L once again. The procurator fiscal decided to hold the murder charge in abeyance, but proceeded with the lost eye and cut hand assault charge.

Jimmy appeared at the sheriff court for a jury trial and was found guilty of the assaults and sentenced to two years. A few months into this sentence, he was taken back to the High Court to face the murder charge. However, witnesses were hard to find and stories of missing witnesses started to appear in the press; it left people fearful of what might happen to them. Then, shortly before the trial, a bomb exploded in the chief prosecution witness's house.

The trial began and there was very little evidence against Jimmy as there were no prosecution witnesses available. The trial was only in its second day when the procurator fiscal offered to accept a not-guilty plea to the murder charge. However, Jimmy pleaded guilty to 'pushing and jostling' and was sentenced to three months.

In January 1966, just after Margaret had given birth to his son, Jimmy was transferred to Peterhead to serve his sentence. He was still only twenty-two years of age and had already amassed a fearful reputation. It was probably because of this that he found himself isolated under the iniquitous Rule 36; he immediately went on a 'dirty' protest and soon found himself consigned to the 'silent cell'.

Jimmy was released from prison in January 1967 and returned to the Gorbals, where he took up with his old associates once again and offered 'protection' to the illegal moneylenders. At the same time, he opened up his own money-lending book as well as operating an illegal drinking racket. Things were now going well for him but, one evening in July 1967, Jimmy went to the house of a man called 'Babs' Rooney who was behind in his payments. In the course of an argument, Jimmy slashed him across the chest, leaving him bleeding severely. When Jimmy left the house, Rooney was still very much alive. The next morning, though, he received the news that Rooney was dead and that the police were busy raiding houses looking for him.

Jimmy, knowing that the police would make every effort to convict him, laid low in Glasgow for a few weeks before moving down to London where the Kray twins, Reggie and Ronnie, arranged a flat for him. He stayed there for two months until armed police raided a pub in East London and caught him sitting having a drink. He was immediately flown back to Glasgow and charged with the murder of 'Babs' Rooney.

The trial began in November 1967 and this time, despite a witness having had his house bombed, he was unanimously found guilty. Lord Cameron sentenced him to life imprisonment with the recommendation that he serve no less than fifteen years.

Jimmy was no sooner back in prison when he had an altercation with a hall governor, punched him in the face and tried to smash him over the head with an inkwell case. He received a severe beating and was forced into a straitjacket before being thrown into a padded cell.

Somehow or other, Jimmy managed to escape from the straitjacket and proceeded to wreck what little there was in the cell, tearing off the heavy canvas covers and stripping the coir stuffing from the walls. He was held in the punishment cells until December 1967, during which time he received news that Margaret had given birth to a daughter. Shortly afterwards, he was taken through to Edinburgh to hear his appeal. The three judges took roughly five minutes to throw it out and Jimmy was escorted straight to Porterfield Prison in Inverness and placed in the punishment cells.

In January 1968, Jimmy was indicted for the assault on the Bar-L governor and was taken under armed escort to Glasgow High Court where he pleaded guilty and received a sentence of eighteen months (added to his life sentence) and returned to Porterfield. He had only been back a few days when he smashed up the governor's office and was immediately flung into the silent cell. Deciding to be as awkward as possible, he began another dirty protest, smearing the walls of his cell and his body with excrement and warning the screws that he would attack them and any governor at every opportunity.

Four months after he arrived at Porterfield, Jimmy was moved to Peterhead, to make room for four rioters who had attacked some screws in the tailor shop there, with one or two of them being badly stabbed in the process. On his first day there, Jimmy punched a screw and was hustled straight down to the punishment block, where he was badly beaten. Refusing to lie down meekly, he fought back and bit a screw in the neck. He found himself on three charges of assault as a result. In retaliation, and in order to strengthen his own defence, Jimmy counter-charged the screws with assaulting him.

In October 1968, Jimmy was tried at Aberdeen High Court on the three assault charges and was found guilty of two of them. He received a further four years and returned directly to Porterfield punishment block where, for almost a year, he continued his running battle with the screws. Things changed in November 1969, when he was refused permission to buy Christmas presents to send to his children. Jimmy attacked a governor, this time spitting on him and trying to force his desk on top of him.

He was removed to a newly built punishment block and thrown into a cell. However, as the building had only recently been built, Jimmy discovered that the cement between the bricks was still relatively soft. He ripped the cover off a ventilator shaft and proceeded to dig out the cement. He broke through to the cell next door within an hour and greeted its surprised occupant with a crazy grin. During the course of the night, and with the digging squad getting bigger every time they broke through a wall, the individual cells became a dormitory. They then began to prepare for the arrival of the morning shift of screws by building a brick barricade across the width of the cells, ready to defy any attempt to move them. The screws attacked them with water hoses and fourteen-pound sledgehammers, before finally subduing them with their long riot sticks and dragging them back to their original punishment cells.

Jimmy was later charged for his attack on the governor and, along with the others, for destroying prison property. He spent six months in solitary without once leaving his cell and, in May 1970, was sentenced to a further six months. He was taken to Peterhead Prison, where he decided to settle down and try and get some sense into his existence.

Things quietened down for over a year, until a man named Bennet, who was serving fifteen years plus a life sentence for stabbing another prisoner in Peterhead, was himself stabbed three times while walking down a corridor. Although there was no evidence that Jimmy had anything to do with the stabbing, once again he found himself in the punishment block on Rule 36. He spent two months there before being allowed back into the prison mainstream.

Early in December 1971, Jimmy received word that his mother had died and he was taken down to Barlinnie under heavy escort so that he could attend her funeral. He was kept handcuffed to two prison officers and armed police surrounded the graveyard – keeping a close eye on both him and the crowd – throughout the entire ceremony. He was returned to Peterhead straight afterwards.

On 4 January 1972, there was a disturbance during the evening recreation when a prisoner went berserk and smashed the hall television sets and other furniture. The following day, Jimmy was dragged out of his cell and taken to the punishment block, where he was assaulted and almost drowned in a sink full of dirty water. He was severely beaten and, when he came to, he found himself in the cages of the segregation unit at Porterfield, buckled into a straitjacket. He spent the next three months there before being returned to Peterhead.

Back in Peterhead, the prisoner Bennet let it be known

that he intended to 'do' Jimmy; it resulted in a pitched battle in the exercise yard that soon developed into a riot. The next day, both Jimmy and Bennet, along with some others, were charged with rioting and assaulting prison officers. Confined to the cellblock, Jimmy found himself confronted one day by Bennet, who had a knife. Jimmy managed to take the knife from Bennet during the fight and stabbed him several times in the chest, puncturing his lung. Later that same day, Jimmy was charged with the attempted murder of Bennet and was returned to Porterfield a few weeks later.

In December 1972, Jimmy appeared at Aberdeen sheriff court – along with the others charged over the yard riot in Peterhead. However, after a legal argument, the sheriff dismissed the charges and Jimmy returned to Porterfield.

Just after Christmas that same month, during a period of association, a riot broke out after Jimmy and four other prisoners attacked the officers on duty in the cages area of Peterhead. One of the screws lost an eye and the others received stab wounds before the prisoners were beaten unconscious. A week later, all the prisoners were charged with the attempted murder of six prison officers. Now Jimmy had two High Court appearances to look forward to: the attempted murder of Bennet and the attempted murder of the six screws at Inverness.

The Bennet case was tried at Aberdeen High Court in January 1973 and Jimmy was happy to be acquitted before being taken back to Inverness. Just over a month later, Jimmy was given his civilian clothes and driven southwards. Not having been told where or why he was going, he was surprised to find himself being driven to Barlinnie Prison, where he was admitted to the often-rumoured, revolutionary special unit. This new unit was designed to give psychiatric support and help to especially difficult prisoners to help them grow into more responsible beings and to show them that there was some light at the end of their long, individual, dark tunnels.

It took Jimmy some time to come to grips with the relaxed regime in the unit and he found it difficult to settle. The knowledge that he would have to return to Porterfield and the cages, and that he was due to stand trial for the riot and attempted murder of the six screws, was always at the back of his mind.

Jimmy was taken back to Porterfield after about three months and, under massive security precautions, including a police helicopter, the trial began. By the end of it, the attempted murder charges had been dropped and the men involved were only found guilty of assault and attempting to escape. They were all sentenced to six years on top. After the trial, Jimmy was returned to the special unit.

Once he had settled properly into the open regime at the unit, Jimmy turned his mind first to clay modelling and then on to sculpting in stone. Mr Richard De Marco, the director of an Edinburgh gallery, praised his work and, within a few years of entering the unit, Jimmy was invited to hold a public exhibition of his work. It was a great success and Jimmy found himself getting commissions, one of which was a giant Gulliver for a children's park.

In 1977, Jimmy's autobiography, *A Sense of Freedom* (Pan), was published; it was an immediate success. Sarah Trevelyan, a psychiatrist, was impressed enough by the book to visit Jimmy in the special unit. Their relationship developed into love and, in 1980, they married at Balfron registry office.

Shortly after his wedding, Jimmy was transferred to Saughton Prison in Edinburgh to complete the final part of his sentence. He was given work in the education unit there and, after about a year, was placed on the Training for Freedom scheme. This meant that he lived in a hostel within the prison but went out to work every day, in his case community social work. He was released not a day before his fifteen-year recommended time was up and went to live in Edinburgh with his wife, Sarah. There, against strong opposition from local residents, Jimmy and Sarah opened a centre for the care of drug addicts and the socially inadequate called The Gateway Exchange. A case of a hard bastard seeing the light at the end of the tunnel.

WULLIE BENNET

Wullie Bennet is, without a doubt, one of the hardest bastards ever to have slept inside Peterhead Prison. He had legendary run-ins with his rival, the aforementioned Jimmy Boyle. Wullie wasn't very well liked back in the old days. Anyway, one day, he went into a cell to fight another very hard prisoner to see who was the top man of their hall: they both got rubbed down to ensure that no knives were used.

Wullie had his knife hanging from a piece of twine, inside his pants. When he entered the cell to fight the man, the door was shut over. Wullie managed to pull his knife from his pants and stabbed the man repeatedly, causing his rival to fall to the cell floor, dead. Wullie didn't panic. Far from it. He pushed the dead convict under the bed in the cell, opened the door and told the man's friends that they could all be pallbearers at the fallen prisoner's funeral. Wullie walked away with his own group of friends: he was sentenced to twenty years on top of his original twelve-year sentence. He was released in the mid-nineties, but is now back inside doing a fifteen-year stretch for kidnapping, shooting and drug offences. His only hope of ever getting back out is by winning his forthcoming appeal. I wish him all the luck in the world, as the man deserves a break.

RONNIE AND BAT NEASON

Ronnie Neason was still a young man when he received his life sentence. He had gained a name for himself outside of prison but, after he arrived in Peterhead, the only thing on Ronnie's mind was to get to the top of the prison pecking order as fast as he possibly could. In Ronnie's case, it only took him two or three short but brutal months, he was so feared. After he had proudly made it to the top of the ladder, he organised sit-in riots and hostages; the screws hated Ronnie so much that they deliberately kept him in their segregation unit for two and three years at a time. The SPS decided that they couldn't afford to have Ronnie walking about their jail causing trouble, so they offered him one of the first spaces in the new Barlinnie special unit to keep him quiet. I'm glad to say that Ronnie is now a free man and that he is doing really well.

Bat Neason is Ronnie's brother. The Bat was doing eighteen years for his part in one of the infamous Hole in the Wall gang's first robberies. After the robbery most of the participants fled, but it wasn't too long before The Bat had been tracked down and sentenced. After completing his sentence he turned to drink for comfort and, one day, was severely slashed down the face by an up-and-coming hard man called John Simpson. I will go into more detail about John later. Bat is still alive and well and has not been back in prison for a long, long time.

FRANK McPHEE

Frank McPhee, as I have already written, was a hard man who came from gypsy stock. He started his life a petty criminal before moving up the pecking order in prison. Most of the other prisoners didn't like Frank when he first arrived in Peterhead, but he never grumbled, kept his head down and proved them all wrong. He became involved in so many riots, hostages and screw stabbings, that the prison system had no alternative but to keep him in seg units for the majority of his sentence.

The time he was allowed out of the segs, he was charged with murdering another prisoner called Worm. Frank and a young boy called Nelly from Edinburgh stood trial and walked for Worm's murder in Perth Prison. After his release, Frank murdered his own best man at his friend's wedding and then went on to cause a war with other heavy gangsters. This hard bastard was eventually brought down by a shot in the head outside his own house by a sniper in the flats some 200–300 metres away. Frank seemed to know he would die a violent death, as he had always talked about it in prison.

'NELLIE' DRUMMOND

No story about Scottish criminals would be complete without mention of big Nellie Drummond. As his nickname implies, Nellie was a well known homosexual, but strangely enough for a person of his inclinations, unpopular in a prison environment, he was well liked and on good terms with most of the 'known' villains. In fact, they knew him on the outside where, on occasion, he had even worked with some of them. On the inside, Nellie was quite brazen about his sexual preferences; on the outside, he remained very much inside the closet.

It was a known fact that Nellie had always been very cooperative with the police whenever he was arrested, but 'the boys' even excused this. The story was always the same: whenever Nellie was arrested for an offence, the police threatened to tell his old mother about his homosexual activities unless he cooperated with them. Most of 'the boys' seemed to think that this excused Nellie's confessions, even if someone else was charged.

'Besides,' someone would always point out, 'everybody knows what Nellie's like, so it's their own fault if they work with him and he sticks them in.'

Big Nellie also got on well with the screws whenever he was in Peterhead (which was quite often). They used to say that you could send two screws off the hall whenever Nellie appeared. On admission to Peterhead's B-Hall, his usual place of residence, Nellie was immediately put in charge of the stores, the cleaning and the hotplate, all of which he organised with the efficiency of a first-class maître d'. What's more, he would always take over the jail bookmaking business, where he applied the same dedication and efficiency, even accepting cash bets from several of the screws.

There are a lot of stories about big Nellie and the things he got up to, and there's no doubt in my mind that Ronnie Barker's Fletch could have learned more than a thing or two from him. He even sold chocolate bars – three for two – as well as trading in banknotes (25p in the pound commission) smuggled in on visits. If Nellie had applied himself on the outside half as much as he did on the inside, he would have been a millionaire in no time. Needless to say, stories about big Nellie are legendary in the Scottish prison system, especially among the older cons, but the two I am about to relate here are among the best.

The first story concerns Nellie's bookmaking dealings. In the days before drugs became the pre-eminent commodity in prison, every jail had a bookie and prisoners would bet with tobacco and would receive their winnings in kind. Credit was a rare commodity offered only to a very few trusted friends, but prisons, harbouring the sort of people they do, were places where nearly everyone was trying to put one over on the bookie. One desperate con spent hours perfecting the insertion of bread into an empty, half-ounce tobacco packet and, one busy Saturday, passed his 'prepared' packet on to Nellie for a half-ounce bet on a horse at odds of 3–1. The horse romped home a clear winner and the grinning con duly entered Nellie's cell to collect his winnings.

'Oh, aye,' said Nellie when the trickster appeared. 'You had that bet on the 3–1 shot, didn't you?'

'Aye.' The conman held out his hand. 'Makes a change to pick a winner, eh?'

Unperturbed, Nellie looked the man straight in the eye and repeated: '3–1, wasn't it?' as he turned away to open his cupboard. 'Right then, I'll just get you your winnings.'

The beaming gambler could hardly contain himself, no doubt already dreaming of an entire weekend puffing away on unlimited roll-ups and perhaps even thinking about swapping a half ounce for a few bars of chocolate to round off his celebrations.

'Right, there you are, that's your stake back,' Nellie handed over the original, doctored half-ounce packet and then, with his face as straight as a die, he counted out three slices of bread into the shattered prisoner's hand.

'And at 3–1, that's your winnings!'

The other story that went the rounds of Peterhead was that, one time, a newcomer, a young, good-looking prisoner, made the mistake of going into Nellie's cell to borrow a couple of LP records.

'Oh, aye, sure, son.' Nellie invited the young chap into his cell. 'You'll find a box of them under the bed. Take a look and see if there's anything you like.'

Then, as the young man bent low to look under the bed, Nellie suddenly grabbed him round the neck in a half-nelson and ripped off the unfortunate fellow's trousers. Now everyone had heard stories about Nellie having a massive member and, personally, I can only go on hearsay, but rumours were rife – Nellie was a big bastard! The story goes that, as Nellie forced himself upon the attractive young man, gripping him tightly round the neck in his favourite wrestling grip while thrusting away at his rear, the lad was heard to scream: 'Oh, oh, stop it! Stop it! You're hurting my neck!'

DUSTER MORRISON

Duster Morrison came from Govan over on Glasgow's very tough Southside. He acquired his nickname when, along with Nellie Drummond he blew a safe that was covered in gelignite. The blast was so powerful that it lifted the young robber off his feet and threw him through a plywood partition into a room full of cardboard boxes that were full of dusters – the name just stuck after that.

When Duster was sentenced to eleven years in the early eighties, he was sent to Barlinnie Prison where he took speed; he consumed far too much, however, went to watch TV in the recreation room, collapsed and died: the speed had blown his heart out; his son, Mo, is very well known in prisons now. I will go into greater detail about young Mo Morrison later in the book.

ALAN BROWN

Alan Brown ran with all the London gangsters before receiving a life sentence for shooting dead a gateman at the Springburn train depot robbery. Alan has now served twenty-eight years of his life sentence – normally, you would have to serve twenty-five, but the prison system refuses to let him out. He went on the run and was only caught a few years ago with £400,000 worth of drugs in his house. However, he has now done his time and should be out of prison.

`JOHNNY BOY´ STEELE

Johnny Boy Steele is the older brother of Joe Steele, the man who was wrongly convicted for the Ice-Cream Wars murders. Johnny has written a book about his wonderfully daring escape attempts and the riots in Peterhead, called *The Bird That Never Flew*; it gives you a good insight into the hard time that Johnny had while serving his sentence. He didn't have one easy day in prison; he stood up to the system the only way he knew how – fighting, fighting and fighting, every single day, until he eventually walked out of prison a free man.

DAVIE COTTERAN

Davie Cotteran received his life sentence along with John Gallagher. They were committing a robbery and, when a man tried to stop them, they stabbed him to death. When a policeman arrived on the scene, he was also stabbed, although not fatally. Davie was the ringleader of the infamous Barlinnie Prison riot and hostage of the late eighties. He got out of prison a couple of years ago, but is now back inside doing seven years. Davie is now in his late fifties and he deserves a chance. He has spent his life in prison like a caged animal.

JOHN GALLAGHER

John Gallagher was Davie Cotteran's co-accused. He spent the first seven years of his life sentence in solitary in one prison or another, as he was a wild young bastard who couldn't be controlled. However, after he entered the Barlinnie special unit, things changed for him. He has been out of prison for going on eight years now and has married and settled down with his wife somewhere in Scotland. Good luck to him.

BILLY FERRIS

Billy Ferris spent twenty-three years of his life sentence in all sorts of prisons up and down Britain. Once he got out, things were looking good until a twist of sadness struck him. Billy is currently serving a second life sentence for the murder of a fifteen-year-old boy. The judge ordered that he serve at least twenty-two of those years behind bars. In defence of Billy, the attack was supposed to have been carried out on the victim's older brother in revenge for an alleged assault on his wife; it was case of mistaken identity. However, I cannot judge and I'm not even going to try.

KENNY KELLY

Kenny Kelly had legendary knife fights in Peterhead Prison with quite a few of the other prisoners. This old-time hood came from Partick in Glasgow and had spent more than thirty-seven years in the prison system. You name it, he had done it. His last sentence, before he took his own life by hanging, was for shooting a man, at point blank, in the face on a Friday night when the pub was at its busiest.

Come on, who in their right mind does that? Why didn't he wait until the man had left the pub? I think Kenny had become institutionalised; before receiving the fifteen years for the pub shooting, he had already served some twenty-odd years behind bars.

While Kenny was inside the penal system, he had a reputation for homosexuality; as a result, he lost the respect of his fellow convicts. It even got to the point where most of the younger prisoners shunned him because of the things he said that he wanted to do to them.

When Kenny was a younger man, he had a violent reputation for going to town with three or four rival gang members. One man in particular – Wullie Bennet –was

Kenny's archenemy. Bennet stabbed Kenny some sixteen times during an infamous cell fight in Peterhead Prison.

Kenny had been going in and out of prison since he was a young man in Glasgow and was a nasty piece of work. Not many liked him; he was also a bully. In his younger days, though, there is no doubt that he was a hard man. Kenny hanged himself on a kids' swing in a park soon after his release from Perth Prison. He was in his late sixties or early seventies.

HUGH COLLINS

Once dubbed Scotland's most dangerous con, Hugh Collins has done his time the hard way. He stabbed three wardens in Perth Prison and took a hostage up in Peterhead before being moved to the special unit in Barlinnie. He spent his time with Jimmy Boyle, from whom he learned to sculpt. After Jimmy Boyle's release, Hugh stuck to it and is now a renowned sculptor in his own right. He has also written the book of his life story, *Autobiography of a Murderer* (Pan, 1997). Best of luck to him.

THOMAS McCULLOCH AND ROBERT MONE

Before I close this rogue's gallery of some of Peterhead's most infamous prisoners, I would just like to give a mention to two other characters: Thomas McCulloch and Robert Mone. They are paired together because they committed their violent crimes together. These two men got sent to the state mental hospital in Carstairs (the Criminal Lunatic Asylum) back in the late sixties, as they both suffered from mental illness.

When they were there, they hatched a plan to escape from the high security hospital. It took them some time to both organise and plan their daring escape attempts after they had befriended an unsuspecting drama teacher, whom they persuaded to help them put on a play. She was bringing old knives and axes and the like into the hospital. She didn't suspect for one minute what the madmen had in store or presumably she would have never brought the stuff in.

Once the knives, axes and chains had been brought in, they were locked in a safe room. However, McCulloch and Mone set about making exact replicas of the weapons out of cardboard. Once these had been completed, they tricked the drama teacher into opening the cupboard, stole the real weapons and replaced them with the cardboard ones. After they had got their incredible bounty back to the ward, well, that was the end of the drama class. The teacher was laid off and the weapons were left in the cupboards untouched. The madmen's plans finally kicked off in late November 1976, when they went on a rampage of murder, killing a nurse and slicing off a patient's ears before cutting his throat.

They then retrieved a rope ladder, which they had previously concealed in the grounds, scaled the fence and got out onto the road. There they waved down a passing police car and when constable George Taylor got out of his vehicle, McCulloch grabbed him by the throat and Mone struck him a blow with a hatchet, killing him instantly. The other constable, John Gillies, made a frantic radio call for help before getting out to try and assist his partner, but the maniacs hijacked his car and drove off into the night.

The pair soon crashed the police car, but they went up to a farmhouse in the country and demanded the keys to the farmer's car. As soon as they had left, Mr Craig, the farmer, phoned the police and reported what had happened. The car was spotted within a few minutes and the police gave chase, capturing the two criminals.

It is interesting to note that, despite the fact that they were patients in Carstairs, presumably on the grounds of insanity, and had escaped, butchering three people in the process, they were still declared sane and fit to plead at their subsequent trial. In which case: what were they doing in Carstairs in the first place?

They were tried at the High Court in Edinburgh and were both sentenced to life imprisonment, with Lord Dunpark, the presiding judge, saying, 'It is plainly no ordinary piece of mindless murder.'

McCulloch was sent to Peterhead where he was, and apparently still is, guarded round the clock in a purpose-built cell in the hospital block which has a complete wall made from reinforced glass – it sounds like Hannibal Lecter's cell – so that he can be closely observed twenty-four hours a day. Mone was sent to Perth, where he is also watched around the clock.

Not long after Mone's incarceration for the three

murders, his elderly father killed three women in Dundee. He is said to have told the police: 'I just wanted to show my boy that I was as good as he was.'

Serving a life sentence for the murder of the three women, Mone Sr was himself stabbed to death by another inmate called Mottan in Craiginches Prison, Aberdeen, while he was working in the cobbler's shop.

McCulloch spent twenty-seven years in total solitary confinement, but not in the way others would have done. He had his own special unit – the same way that the Lockerbie bomber has – above the surgery in Peterhead's convict prison. Known to all the prisoners as the 'Birdman of Peterhead', he is the longest-serving prisoner in the jail's history.

No longer in his solitary unit, he is hoping for release so that he can walk the streets of Scotland once again. He was recently moved to HM Prison Saughton, down in Edinburgh, to further both his progress and his chances of release back into the community.

One last thing before I close this chapter. I would like to mention some other prisoners: Larry Winters (Bally) died while he was in the special unit at Barlinnie; Andy Gentels hung himself in Greenock Prison, no one knows why; and, of course, the most infamous prisoner of them all: TC Campbell, a man who is innocent and who was wrongly convicted of six murders. TC is currently going through an appeal to clear his name. I wish you all the best. I'd also like to show my respect to Larry Bally and old Andy, both of whom never made it to the end of their sentences. God bless you both.

JAMES CROSBIE

James Crosbie, author of *It's Criminal* (John Blake Publishing, 2004), was born on 15 January 1937 into a respectable, working-class, Roman Catholic family and was the middle of three brothers. James didn't get into serious trouble until 1954 when, at the age of seventeen, he appeared in front of the sheriff court on charges of stealing and was sentenced to two years' probation.

In September 1954, he joined the RAF under the delusion that everyone in the RAF got to fly about in aeroplanes. He soon discovered his mistake and, as a regular airman, exercised his option of buying himself out. He was in minor breach of his probation on two or three occasions and, in February 1955, was sentenced to four years' borstal training for breaking into and stealing from an office. James served two years in Polmont borstal, Scotland, and, when released, was immediately called up for National Service.

In 1957, he appeared at Aldershot magistrates' court for stealing an officer's car and was sentenced to six months. When he was released from Wandsworth Prison in 1958, he failed to return to his unit and started to live in London.

In 1958, James appeared at the County of London sessions and was sentenced to three years' corrective training on charges of receiving stolen property (it didn't work!). A year after his release from Maidstone Prison, he appeared at the Old Bailey and was charged, along with Jack Witney (who, in 1966, was later sentenced to life imprisonment for the murder, by shooting, of three flying-squad detectives) and two other men, with conspiracy to rob, along with two further charges of possessing offensive weapons. This time the sentence was three-and-a-half years.

On leaving prison, James travelled to Ghana, West Africa, where he stayed with a relative who was the manager of a cocoa mill in the coastal town of Takoradi. He finally returned to Glasgow in 1965 and, later on the same year, was sentenced to eighteen months for attempting to break into a bank in Riddrie, Glasgow. He was released from Peterhead in April 1966 and got married on 5 November the same year. By now he had started a small wrought-iron business and was doing very well, until an offence from his past caught up with him and, in late 1967, he was sentenced to eighteen months.

When James was released in 1968, he returned to his wrought-iron shop and worked successfully for several years. He took flying lessons during this time and became a pilot. He also took extra courses at Southend airport where he trained on larger, twin-engine aircraft. In the meantime, his business was growing to such an extent that he bought a small factory and expanded into manufacturing furniture. In 1971, he expanded still further, renting a large main-street shop in Springburn Road, Glasgow, retailing furniture, which he imported himself from Germany. By now his family, consisting of his wife Margaret and his son Gregory, who was born in July 1969, had moved into a semi-detached house in the Bishopbriggs suburb.

On 23 May 1972, James and an accomplice carried out an armed raid on the Clydesdale Bank, Hillington, and stole over £65,000 – a record haul for a bank robbery in Scotland.

On 30 April 1974, James and another accomplice raided the Clydesdale Bank at Whiteinch and stole £87,000 – another new record for a bank robbery in Scotland. About two months later, James was arrested and charged with the Whiteinch robbery and was remanded to Barlinnie Prison. As a result of a blunder by the police, he was given bail and promptly disappeared before they could charge him with the robbery at Hillington. Two months later, on 8 August 1974, James single-handedly held up a branch of the Royal Bank of Scotland in Edinburgh and stole £17,000 – still the biggest amount stolen by a lone bank robber in Scotland.

Two days later, when attempting to get out of Edinburgh, he was spotted by two Glasgow detectives and was arrested as he walked out of a shop.

At the High Court in Edinburgh, the judge, Lord Robertson, took note that James had failed to cooperate with the police by naming his accomplices and had not returned any of the stolen money. Telling James that, in his opinion, he was the most dangerous man in Scotland, Lord Robertson sentenced him to twenty years.

During the first year of his sentence, James made two escape attempts – by sawing through his window bars – but he never made it over the wall. He was kept on 'A' category for over three years before he was allowed to attend education classes or go out onto the outer yard to watch the prison football matches.

During his time in Peterhead, James took up writing. In his first attempt at the annual Koestler Awards Scheme, he won first prize in both the novel and playwriting categories he had entered. He also attended education classes and passed about six O-levels, three Highers and gained two distinctions when passing the HNC Certificate in business studies.

In all, James served a total of twelve years and eight months before his release. On leaving prison, he gained a place at Glasgow University to study the BA course in English and Scottish literature and passed his first year in the top ten per cent of the class.

In 1988, James bought a television set and a video recorder using false details to obtain credit. He was arrested for this and was sentenced to three years for fraud. His university aspirations had come to an abrupt end.

On finishing the three years, James moved out to Spain and lived there until he was arrested at Dover in 1993 for smuggling 20kg of cannabis into the country. He was sentenced to eighteen months at Maidstone Crown Court and served most of his sentence at Stamford Hill Prison on the Isle of Sheppey.

James returned to Spain on his release and continued operations there until, in 1996, he was caught at Birmingham airport carrying 50kg of cannabis. This time he appeared at Warwick Crown Court and was sentenced to four-and-a-half years. He spent his sentence as constructively as he could, bringing his total of Koestler certificates up to nine and passing an A-level course in creative writing.

On his release from Haverigg Prison, James returned to Glasgow and got married for the second time, to a woman called Marlene. In 2001, while waiting to board a ship bound for Iceland from the west coast of Scotland, James was arrested by HM Customs. They found him wearing a corset of cannabis, wrapped around his body. He was given eight years, where he went on to gain yet more Koestlers – he now has a total of fourteen.

After winning parole, James saw his life story, *It's Criminal*, serialised in the Scottish *News of the World*. A talented writer, he's currently living in Glasgow, working hard on his writing and has written film scripts, one of which is based on the English prisoner Charles Bronson's life. James has also written some crime thrillers: *Ashanti Gold* and *Payday for Some*, which he hopes to have published. He has also written numerous short stories of great anecdotal strength. Good luck, James.

3

Scottish Hard Female

`BIG MAGS´

Not all Scottish hard bastards are male! The females of the species are also forces to be reckoned with, and few come more redoubtable than Margaret 'Big Mags' Haney Young. With convictions going back to the seventies for assault, breach of the peace, fraud and contempt of court, Big Mags sat proudly at the top of her criminal family's network for over fifteen years, until she received a twelve-year sentence at the High Court in April 2003.

In June 2001, Big Mags, from Clackmannanshire, faced drug charges at Stirling sheriff court along with six members of her family, all of whom were charged with dealing in heroin. Without ceremony, fifty-eight-year-old Big Mags was remanded and accused of being connected with the supply of heroin in the town's Lower Bridge Street between 1 and 8 January 2001, where the drugs were cut in the morning before being put into bundles of ten wraps and distributed through a system of runners with Mags acting as the controller.

Along with Big Mags, her daughter, granddaughter,

former husband, two nieces and daughter-in-law appeared on the same charge – the whole clan: Diane Haney, 33; Lynette McGowan, 18; John Haney, 70; Roseanne Haney, 38, and Mary Haney, 35, all from Stirling; and Anne Morrison, 29, of Deanston in west Perthshire. All had their bail applications refused.

When it came to the plea when they appeared individually and in private before Sheriff Roddy McLeod, all seven withheld their decision and were committed for further examination.

The trial of the notorious Haneys took place in March 2003, after four family members entered guilty pleas to supplying heroin on a large scale. First was the family matriarch, Big Mags: she pleaded guilty during her trial at the High Court.

Along with her, her daughter Diane, son Hugh, and niece Roseanne Haney, also pleaded guilty. Mags' former husband, John Haney, walked free from the dock after his plea of not guilty to drug dealing was accepted. Diane Haney was described as a key player, Hugh was a runner and Roseanne was Diane's 'co-pilot'. Diane was formerly known as Mandy and, in 1997, revealed that her mother had got her addicted to heroin. She returned to her family a few years later as Diane Raploch.

The prosecution put it to the court that Mags and her co-accused had sought to establish a drugs empire in Stirling, mainly from flats at Lower Bridge Street, which acquired the nickname 'Haney's Hotel'. As is normally the case, the prosecution put the knife in when the court was told that Mags received £1,200 a month in benefits;

they wanted to show how small this amount was in comparison to her turnover in drugs cash.

The prosecution used every conceivable weapon in their toolbox to make Mags look like a drug baroness and they estimated that she could make £200 to £300 a day from dealing. And if that wasn't enough to blacken the already besmirched character of Mags, it was put to the court that she also acted as a fence when she exchanged drugs for stolen property, giving thieves £10 or £20 for items to buy heroin from her.

Because of their guilty pleas, the prosecutor, Drew Mackenzie, didn't need to call the star witness. He made reference to whoever it was, however, by saying: 'Another witness, who would have given evidence, said that Big Mags sat in her house like the Queen... and they thought they were untouchable.'

In April 2003, at the High Court in Edinburgh, the four guilty members of the Haney family were given jail sentences totalling thirty-three years for large-scale heroin dealing: Mags was given twelve years, her daughter Diane was sentenced to nine, her niece Roseanne to seven and her son Hugh to five. Would you believe it, Mags' granddaughter, Kim, was also jailed for two years for contempt after her refusal to appear as a prosecution witness in the trial against the clan.

The judge described the victims of the heroin trade who appeared in court to give evidence at the trial of the Haneys as 'ghosts'.

On the estimate that Mags had been selling between £400–£1,000-worth of heroin a day, the court adjudged that she must a have been involved in the sale of hundreds of thousands of pounds worth of heroin over an eighteen-month period.

With this in mind, the Crown wanted its pound of flesh. In my opinion, the Crown is no better than a drug dealer; they both want the profits from drug dealing to line their own purse. The Crown said it was entitled to pursue only her 'realisable assets', which apparently included mundane items such as a caravan. In instances like this, the Crown will only think about one thing: she laundered the profits through her family. However, there were no confiscation proceedings against other members of her family. At the time of Mags' arrest, police only managed to seize £10,740 in cash. After her conviction, the Crown confirmed that it had identified realisable assets with a total estimated value of £11,425.

The Haneys ran their drugs empire on the Raploch Estate in Stirling, until they were chased out by a 400-strong mob in 1997. That is when Mags launched a renewed, and much more significant, drugs business from Lower Bridge Street in the city.

Anyone recalling the Dunblane massacre, when Thomas Hamilton allegedly went berserk on the morning of 13 March 1996 after walking into the Dunblane Primary School, may recall a Christmas song, which I think was based on the Vietnam victims' song 'Knocking On Heaven's Door'. Well, it was only a matter of time before the Stirling police gave Alan Christie's name to the Scottish *Daily Mail*. What was so infamous about

Christie that it warranted such drastic action by the police? Alan Christie had just served a year's prison sentence for molesting a four-year-old girl!

By now, a lynch-mob, headed by Big Mags, had turned 'Knocking On Heaven's Door' to 'Hammering On A Paedophile's Door', when they marched to his lodgings in Stirling screaming: 'Beast out!' Appearing on the TV news that night, Big Mags was seen using a child's microphone loudspeaker system to amplify her chants of: 'Beast out! Beast out!' All that could be seen was a hooded man, obviously Christie, being led away down the stairs and into a waiting car, before being whisked away to a place of safety. What Big Mags did took some guts; she did what the others feared to do, but she garnered their spirit and led the way – the others duly followed. You can never take that away from Mags. Call her what you will, but she had to be a hard bastard to go ahead and do that.

In October 2003, appearing at the appeal court and looking a shadow of her former anti-paedophilic self and now using a walking stick, the judges were told that she was undergoing radiotherapy and chemotherapy for cervical cancer. Her defence solicitor-advocate, Pat Wheatley, said that no information was available on the long-term prognosis. He argued that, although Haney's crime deserved a substantial jail sentence, it should be less than twelve years.

The appeal judges rejected the appeal. The cancer-stricken Mags claimed that her sentence was excessive. The three other members of her crime family also appealed against their sentences. All of the appeals were rejected when Scotland's second most senior judge, Lord Gill, said at the Court of Criminal Appeal in Edinburgh: 'We consider each of these sentences to be amply warranted by the facts.'

Mags seemed to attract trouble wherever she went. The Raploch Estate in Stirling was a nice, working-class environment in which to live and to bring up your kids. Then the scourge of drugs took a grip of its sons and daughters. The more people needed drugs, the rougher and more violent the place became.

Most, if not all, of the working-class families moved out of the area after their properties became the target of drug-induced men and women. Because of the famous Wallace Monument and castle, Stirling attracts tourists from all over the world. These numbers increased when the film *Braveheart*, starring Mel Gibson, hit the big screens all over the world.

The junkies had a field day; they didn't care one jot for the safety of the overseas tourists and would stop at nothing. Some tourists were left bloodied and battered on the sacred ground of the Wallace Monument, minus their video cameras and the like. The cameras were soon sold to a fence in the Raploch for pennies, compared to the actual price it was worth and the junkies didn't waste much time getting to Big Mags's door with the £20 they had received.

This behaviour went on and on and, as time went by, more and more young men would start doing even more reckless acts of violence to gain some money to buy their heroin from Mags or from her daughter or from another family member. At the height of her power, Mags and her family were responsible for supplying most of Stirling with their daily fix of heroin. The people in Stirling who hated drugs and what they stood for got together to rally round Mags' front door, shouting for the whole family to be evicted from the Raploch Estate: it didn't take long before they got their wish.

The council moved in with the local police to remove them from the house they had lived in all their lives. It didn't have much effect. They soon set up shop in another part of Stirling. However, they didn't know that the police had started a major surveillance operation. After some many months of constant surveillance, the drug squad raided Mags' house and the houses of her family.

Mags is now in her early sixties and if she makes it to the end of her sentence she will be seventy-two years old, unless she behaves herself and wins early release; however, she only has limited chances of surviving the cervical cancer.

I am not going to comment on the sad state of affairs that befell Big Mags and her clan, as there are plenty worse people that the police could have turned their attention to, like rapists and monsters who harm children. Mags led a full community back in the early nineties to remove a convicted sex beast who had been placed in the Raploch, right next to a primary school. People seem to forget that Big Mags did good deeds in her community as well; she was always helping people out with money so that they could feed their children. Some may say it was drug money, but nearly every £20 note in circulation in

Scotland has been in one drug dealer's hand or another. It is just a shame that her own kind had turned on her when, just a year or so earlier, she had been their champion spokesperson and local charity.

Not a lot of people want to remember that side of Big Mags and her infamous crime clan. I just hope that Mags wins her toughest battle of all against the cancer and walks out of the front gates of Cornton Vale a free woman. It doesn't matter what anyone thinks or says about Big Mags; she doesn't deserve to die in prison of cancer. No way is that right, in anyone's language.

Just out of interest, in April 2003, Edinburgh granny Barbara Donaldson appeared on court in drug-dealing charges after police found eleven bags of heroin hidden in her socks and sleeves when they raided the neighbourhood café she was running.

The High Court in Edinburgh was told that Donaldson dealt the class-A drug to customers at the Bargo Cafe in Gracemount during working hours, between 6 October 2001 and 6 February 2002. In her defence, Donaldson told the police that she had bought the drugs on behalf of her drug-addict daughter and that she intended to supply her with two wraps a day to help wean her off heroin.

Her lawyer, John Keenan, told the court that she had only started selling the heroin when she encountered financial difficulties and that she was using the money she received to buy drugs for her daughter. The court was also told that Donaldson was looking after eight grandchildren under the age of sixteen: two were the children of a daughter who committed suicide; three were the children of the daughter who is currently on methadone; and three the children of a third daughter, who is serving six months in Cornton Vale women's prison.

In late April 2003, after the judge, Lady Cosgrove, had deferred sentence on Donaldson for the preparation of a background report, Donaldson was sentenced to eighteen months' imprisonment. In October of the same year, housing chiefs evicted her from her home as a result of her anti-social behaviour.

The defence counsel's earlier please for clemency fell on deaf ears after the court was told that Donaldson had become so well known as a dealer that her business had become known in the trade as 'Smackdonalds'. Insiders have described Donaldson as a 'nasty piece of work' and have warned her not to return to the area because of a feared backlash from her local community.

Sentencing Donaldson, Lady Cosgrove said that a community service sentence was not an appropriate punishment for dealing in class-A drugs.

So there you have it: one granny gets twelve years and one gets eighteen months; it proves that notoriety attracts a more punitive sentencing from the courts. The bigger the name, the harder the fall. Good luck, Big Mags.

4

The Taxman

BRIAN COCKERILL

While I'm mentioning drug dealers, I have to mention a man who is hated by the peddlers of the soul-destroying stuff. Big Brian 'The Taxman' Cockerill (aka Scots Brian) was born on 16 December 1964 in Coatbridge, Lanarkshire. At 6ft 3in, with 23st of rock-solid muscle, his awesome power has made him a truly terrifying force in Britain's underworld. A walking colossus, anyone who gets in his way and tries to stay there had better be ready for the hiding of their life. For, although Brian can be polite, woe betide anyone who mistakes that politeness for weakness. Someone of Brian's stature only comes along once in 100 years; he is one of the hardest bastards on the planet.

Over the last two decades, Brian has ruled his world with an iron fist. Using nothing but his hands as weapons, he has patrolled the streets, clubs and raves of Britain in order to keep order and to 'tax' those whose ill-gotten gains he sees fit to take his share of. Drug dealers and shady club promoters everywhere know that if The

Taxman is in town, it's time to pay up or get out. All of them are fully aware of the appalling violence this man can exert on his enemies and of the incredible presence of both body and mind that he possesses.

His story is one of unbridled violence, of legendary fighting and of devastating personal victories. Yet despite his appalling record of aggression, Brian is a man who lives by rules and respect – balanced yet unpredictable, he has never used weapons, and those who have used arms against him have barely lived long enough to regret it. He's hard, yet fair, and the facts of his life are as amazing and awe-inspiring as they are true.

Brian once said: 'I remember the police once asking me why I was called the Taxman. I sarcastically told them that the Chancellor of the Exchequer was the taxman, even though I was wearing a T-shirt emblazoned with the words: "The No. 1 Taxman".'

Britain's authorities have behaved like gangsters for centuries, yet their crimes are always swept under the carpet. The UK is drowning in a sea of illegal drugs, more so than at any time known to man. Most crime stems from its birthplace in the murky world of drugs: smackheads and crackheads waiting near post offices to mug old ladies for a few pounds from their handbags and people intent on turning over other vulnerable members of the community for whatever else they can get. All this just so they can get their £5 fix! Brian says:

> I can't do anything about every single junkie that
> blights their community in the UK, as I'm only

one man. However, blitzing the source of the street urchins' drug supply means the drug dealer gets it! Forget about these academics, community groups and government organisations – they do nothing to help eradicate drug users or to help the parents. There are thousands of organisations throughout the world whose sole aim is to cut down drug use, all in receipt of big money.

Let's face it: drugs are here to stay – legal and illegal. The tax revenue from legal drugs has brought billions of pounds into the coffers of the bloodsucking British government. Look at the way we're all taxed from the cradle to the grave and then tell me if that isn't the truth about this mob of Westminster gangsters. They're leeches that cream off our hard-earned cash.

What's the difference between the government and a gangster? A gangster gives you a choice, whereas the government didn't! Look at it this way: a gangster will tax businesses for protection money. The nightclub boss pays a few grand a week for the services of the local muscle. Any trouble that flares is quelled and the troublemakers are hunted down, one by one. Now, if the nightclub boss phones the police, they might turn up, but there's no guarantee that they'll get the matter resolved. And, when you consider how much the club boss has forked out to the local council in taxes, he gets fuck all for his money!

The police don't know whether to vilify Brian or to recommend him for a knighthood; the senior officers hate him and put propaganda out about him; the junior ranks love him because of what he does.

In 2007, Brian will be running for the position as mayor of Middlesbrough, one that is currently held by ex-'Robocop' Ray Mallon, who won the position despite having resigned in disgrace from Teesside police force after admitting to fourteen internal charges: he was reprimanded on one of them, cautioned on two and forced to resign on the remainder. So if Mallon can win the seat of mayor, surely Brian can as well.

Brian's book, *The Taxman* (John Blake Publishing, 2005), tells his full story and he is currently working on a follow-up. In the meantime, if The Taxman taps you on the shoulder, give him his dues or else say your prayers... just don't offer him drugs.

5

Nut Jobs

Some hard bastards go about their business with total self-control; others rely on an element of unpredictability to get their message across. And then you have those who are dangerous bastards because they have not a shred of sanity, often as a result of the nightmare they've experienced behind the bars of Scottish prisons.

STEVIE ANDERSON

Stevie Anderson, a lifer with a reputation for violence, came from Paisley, just outside of Glasgow. When he arrived in Perth Prison, word soon got around that he was going to have a dash at the little gang of hardened criminals who were running the halls at the time.

It didn't take them long to approach Stevie, but he was having none of the rival criminals' shit. He dragged one of them into his cell and stabbed him repeatedly. After a very nasty incident, Stevie was brought to Glenochil Prison, where he was placed in the same segregation unit as his rival, Andy McCann.

It wasn't long before they were at each other's throats, day in, day out, over something that had happened in Shotts Prison some years beforehand. Sooner or later one of them would make their move.

Unfortunately, Stevie was caught on the hop when he was in the shower. As I described earlier, the screws left the door open, probably deliberately but, to be fair to Andy McCann, he didn't know that the shower door was open until he walked by on his way to the phone. After seeing the unlocked door, Andy went back to his cell and got his piece of steel – the rest is history.

Stevie returned from the Stirling Royal Infirmary and was let up into the mainstream; he proceeded to get on well with everyone, until he took it upon himself to steal a parcel of heroin from a friend of mine.

Stevie knew my friend wouldn't do anything about it, but he was in for a shock. I was neither impressed by nor scared of Stevie, despite his formidable reputation for violence. I approached him and asked for the heroin back. In reply, he told me that I wasn't getting it because he had already done most of it and the little bit he had left, he was saving for his breakfast the next morning.

I walked away in silent fury. I got a lock-back knife that one of my pals was holding for another mutual friend with only one thing on my mind: to stick it as far as I could into Stevie's chest. That is exactly what I did.

I think Stevie was more shocked that a young boy of twenty-two years of age – me at the time – had the nerve and audacity to stab him multiple times. After I stabbed him, he went back to hospital and then back to the prison, where he went on to be stabbed a further seventeen times, by two different men on different occasions.

Following the last of those stabbings, he was placed in the seg unit and lay there for ten months. Out of the blue, the governor went in and told Stevie that he was being transferred up to Perth Prison. He accepted the move happily and, unbeknown to the screws, was given a 10in knife from another prisoner. The prisoner Sellotaped the knife to Stevie's back to evade detection when he was searched in the reception area of Glenochil before he left on route to Perth.

When they were in the jail van, Stevie was cuffed to a screw by his left hand. However, he slipped his right hand up the back of his sweatshirt and pulled the 10in knife from its secure binding. Once it was tightly in his hand, he flashed it before the screws. They tried to jump on him, but to no avail. Stevie started stabbing and slashing the three screws who were escorting him to Perth. He stabbed two of them, inflicting severe injuries; the other warden was slashed down the arms and hands.

Stevie now had complete control of the van; his only downfall was that he couldn't drive, so he threatened the civilian driver to pull off the motorway and take him back to Glasgow. The driver panicked.

When he pulled off the motorway, the driver realised he was in Perth and, instead of turning the jail van round and returning to Glasgow, crashed the van straight into the gates of Friarton semi-open prison. The game was up for Stevie: he was overpowered, receiving horrific injuries in the process.

He didn't receive any medical treatment. Instead, he was taken back to Glenochil seg unit, where he was kept on Cat A for three full years and received an extra seven years at Forfar High Court for his escape bid. At court, he told the PF (procurator fiscal) that he had done the screws in the van to get back at them for leaving the shower door open for Andy McCann to stab him. Fair play. However, after he got back into mainstream, his head was totally messed up.

The screws in Glenochil seg unit had played one mind game after the other on Stevie until it took its toll on his mind; he lasted only four days in mainstream prison before he cut his own penis with a razor blade. It was the last time that Stevie was seen in prison. He went up to Carstairs state mental hospital and remains there to this day. After all he has been through, he has recently been told that he has got MS.

Even though I had a run-in with this man, I still wish him all the best. I really hope that he can get back out of Carstairs some time in the near future, be it back in prison or, preferably, as a free man. He has now been inside for some nineteen years, so he has more than served his time.

GARY SIMPSON

I have known Gary Simpson since I was fifteen years of age. I have also seen with my own eyes some of the things he has done. When Gary and I were in Greenock young offenders back in 1988, Gary had a few run-ins with the so-called 'top boys' of the institute.

Gary was alone at the time and, after Greenock was turned into an adult prison, he won, against all the odds. Gary and I, along with some thirty other young prisoners, were transferred to Dumfries young offenders – a place with a reputation for being the most violent young offenders' institute in Scotland.

When I arrived there, two or three days before Gary, the talk among all the Glasgow young up-and-coming hard men was of how they were going to stab and murder Gary Simpson. They weren't kidding either: most of them had just been sentenced to life in prison for murder, so they were up for anything. To add fuel to the fire, a boy with a reputation for violence had been stabbed and murdered some two months before we left Greenock young offenders.

Things didn't take long to get going. When Gary, the top man of Greenock young offenders, walked into Dumfries, he was met by a mob who told him that he wasn't the daddy and that he should do what they say.

You all know what is coming. Gary got himself a jail knife, marched into the recreation hall and challenged them all to a fight. No one took him up on the challenge. The other mob planned a nasty fight when they got back to the hall, but Gary heard of the plans and didn't give them a chance to attack him mob-handed.

He stabbed one of the top boys and then carried on smashing the other rivals' heads with a battery that he had hidden down his trousers in a sock. This little turf war went on and on for over a year but, to Gary's credit, he emerged from it unscathed. So much so, in fact, that he declared himself the top boy, much to the horror of all the other so-called hard men.

You will get a better picture of what I mean from watching the film *Scum* (1979, starring Ray Winstone), because that was exactly the way it happened. It was one boy's struggle against a group of boys. After Gary left the young offenders, he went to Perth Prison and was placed next to the by-now hated and feared Robert Matton. It didn't seem to bother Gary: he walked into Matton's cell and smashed him over the head with his flask of hot water. When Gary got camped up with Joe Boyle, another one of the prison's hated men, it was Goodnight Vienna.

Despite the fact that most people who were around at the time have heard of or have seen the violence Gary and Joe did to all-comers, Gary ended up in the state mental hospital. When this happened, people started to diss both him and his reputation, openly calling him a mongo and the like. To be fair to Gary, though, not many have called him such things to his face.

I am not trying to stick up for him. I am only writing a true account of what I have seen and heard with my own eyes and ears. Nowadays, people say that he is finished as a man of violence. I don't want to comment one way or the other, but if a boy can fight a whole prison population on his own, be the top doorman in pubs and clubs at twenty-one years of age and chap guys' doors and shoot them at point-blank range with a 9mm before walking away laughing, he surely is, deep down, a very dangerous man and a true hard bastard.

'LINKY' LYNAS

John 'Linky' Lynas also has a reputation for being a very hard man. He was one of the most prolific bank robbers of his generation, robbing banks up and down the length of Britain. I was in a children's home with Linky and his two brothers when we were little kids. He left the home and I didn't come across him again until we met in Glenochil; he was doing thirteen years for yet another bank robbery and had just been brought up from England.

Once we were settled into Glenochil, the screws kept trying to be smart with him. He eventually lost his temper and smashed up three screws in their office, breaking two of their jaws. Linky was then taken to the seg unit, where he embarked on another personal battle with the screws; not to go out and beat them up or stab them, but to make sure that he was returned to mainstream. However, Linky was considered far too dangerous to allow that to happen.

Over a nine-month period, the screws jaded Linky with all sorts of shit, placing tablets in his food and playing with his head. It would have broken some of the hardest prisoners but, to his credit, Linky kept on at them until, one day, they jagged some drugs into his body and put him to sleep.

He woke up in Carstairs mental hospital, where he remained for some three years. I can now happily say that John 'Linky' Lynas is back in mainstream prison. He is off his medication and has not needed to turn to violence to present his point of view. I really pity the prisoner or screw that rubs Linky up the wrong way though, as he is by far the most explosive man I know. Don't ever be fooled by his happy-go-lucky attitude.

BABA KILPATRICK

Baba Kilpatrick started off doing thirteen years for his part in an armed robbery. His co-accused was Joe Boyle and they were charged with having robbed the rent offices in Govan, Glasgow. When Baba went to Perth Prison, he kept his head down and got on with his sentence. He wasn't a first offender though, far from it: he had been coming in and out of prison since he was a frail sixteen-year-old boy.

This sentence was different for him, however, as he had never done more than three years before. He now found himself in the major league of crime. Baba kept his head down until he became rather friendly with Cop McKewan and Rab Raker, who had ideas about planning a riot and taking the screws hostage. Well, like any other young boy, Baba didn't need to be asked twice. He sat, day after day, with Cop and Rab, talking about how they would do the riot and how they would get the screws. However, as I have already stated, most of the best-laid plans go pear-shaped and this one was no different.

They did, however, riot and managed to get hold of a screw: they didn't take him hostage, though; all they wanted were his keys – on the flat below them were forty of Scotland's worst monsters, most of who were waiting to move to Glenochil, where most of the worst sex-case convicts were held before 1991, when the SPS decided to turn Peterhead into a beasts' paradise. Up until that time, there had never been a prison solely for rapists in the history of Scotland's penal system.

Baba, Cop and Rab played a very big part in them getting their own prison: after they had chased all of the screws out of the hall, they headed straight for the monsters' flat and opened doors at random. Even though the beasts may have heard the commotion going on outside in the hall, they were powerless to do anything about it.

Once the three knife-wielding, masked prisoners entered their cells, the monsters knew that their tea was out. Baba, Cop and Rab stabbed, slashed and scalded over twelve of the worst sex-case convicts as a form of prison justice: I can only pat them on the back every time I see them for their actions. If there were more prisoners in the system like these three men, the jails would be better places and it might send the right message to these offenders: perhaps they wouldn't have committed their sickening crimes in the first place if they had known about what had happened to their monster friends. Sadly, there aren't many other prisoners like Baba, Cop and Rab.

They saved their most spectacular show of prison justice until the end. The beast was a man from Dundee. When his cell door was opened he tried to make a dash for freedom, but there was no way he was getting away from the boys. They dragged him back into his cell and beat him semi-conscious before tying him to a mattress... and then set fire to both the mattress and to him.

When the boys were happy that the monster had been set alight, they pulled him out of the cell and flung him off the third floor – some 30ft – onto the concrete floor of the hall below. One of the riot screws put out the beast's by-now burnt and crispy clothes with a fire hose. He received over seventy per cent burns to his body... In my view, he should have burned alive for what he did to that little girl in Dundee.

When the riot came to an end, Baba, Cop and Rab were removed to Peterhead's most infamous seg unit, and they stayed there until their High Court trial. Baba got seven years, Cop got twelve years on top of his lifer and Rab got thirteen years on top of his lifer. Baba has now finished his twenty years, but sadly he is back in doing another seven-year stretch. Cop is still in prison; he did manage to escape and have sex with a woman prison warden who had fallen in love with him before he was, sadly, returned. He is now in a wheelchair.

Last, but no means least, Rab is still inside as well. He married the social worker he met in Shotts special unit, but the marriage was short-lived. When Rab went to Saughton Prison in Edinburgh, his local prison, he got into a heated argument with a boy, Eddie, from Fife who had a bit of a temper on him. Eddie had just been sentenced to thirteen years himself and wasn't going to back down from Rab. He didn't like the way that Rab was trying to talk to his friend, Stevie. The two boys decided to teach Rab a lesson; he was found lying in a pool of his own blood after having been stabbed over twenty-three times – it was a miracle that he survived the frenzied attack. The doctors in hospital had to open him up and give him over eighteen pints of blood, but he made a recovery and successfully sued the prison service for negligence: he was awarded seven grand. I would just like to say big ups to you all.

6

Loch Ness
Monsters

I have heard the words 'beasts', 'monsters' and 'sex cases' ever since I first went to prison. At first I couldn't quite understand why grown, hairy-arsed men in the cell area of the busiest court in Britain would shout these kinds of words at other prisoners. However, it didn't take me long to understand that the hardened prisoners were venting their anger at the men who had raped or murdered children, girls, young boys, women or old ladies. After being told what they had done, it didn't take too long before I too was hanging out of the cell bars calling such sub-humans every horrible word that I knew. Now I don't believe in the death penalty for normal domestic, or gang fight, murders, but I do believe in hanging beasts like Huntley, Whiting, Brady, Black and co., as they have been found guilty of the worst crimes known to man.

This chapter will, I hope, highlight some of Scotland's worst-ever monsters, perverts, serial killers and unspeakable bastards. Some of them are currently doing their time in England; others have since died. Good.

PETER THOMAS ANTHONY MANUEL

The last person to be hanged in Glasgow, at the age of just thirty-one, was a criminal by the name of Peter Thomas Anthony Manuel. He swung from the gallows in Barlinnie Prison on 11 July 1958.

Born in New York of Scottish parents in 1927, the family returned to Scotland in 1932. At first, his family settled in Motherwell but, within a few years, they moved south and set up home in Coventry. In 1941, they were bombed out of their home in Coventry and returned to Uddingston, in Lanarkshire, Scotland.

Peter Manuel gained his first conviction in 1938 at the age of eleven. By the time he was thirteen, he had collected his third conviction and was sentenced to approved school. His first arrest was for burglary at Coventry in October 1939. Five weeks later, he was packed off to reform school on a charge of housebreaking.

He spent most of his youth, up to the age of eighteen, in approved schools and borstal, mostly for housebreaking and committing brutal assaults with weapons such as hammers and knives. He was also suspected of many assaults on women in his area, but was never charged. During his many court appearances, Manuel often defended himself and was complimented by the judge on more than one occasion for his handling of the case.

By 1942, Manuel had committed his first sexual offence on the wife of a school employee. He was jailed for the offence and was released two years later. In March 1946, he was convicted on fifteen counts of housebreaking and was sentenced to prison. While serving his time, he was also convicted of rape and received a further eight years.

In 1946, he was sentenced to eight years on a serious assault and attempted murder charge. During this sentence, he was charged on two occasions with attacks on prison officers and received further sentences.

Over a four-year period, from 1954 to 1958, Manuel killed seven people in and around Glasgow and the Lowlands area of Scotland using a Webley revolver, a Beretta pistol and an iron bar.

On 4 January 1956, he bludgeoned a young girl, Anne Knielands, aged 17, to death with a brick and left her body on a golf course. Again in 1956, he broke into the Watt family bungalow and fatally shot Mrs Watt, her daughter Vivienne and Mrs Watt's sister, Margaret Brown. In Newcastle, on 8 December 1956, he shot and killed a taxi driver, Sydney Dunn. During 1957, he shot and killed a girl, Isabelle Cooke, aged 17, and, on 6 January 1958, he broke into the Smart family bungalow and murdered, by shooting, Mr and Mrs Smart, along with their eleven-year-old son.

Tried at the High Court, Manuel sacked his counsel halfway through the case and, once again, took on his own defence. He was found guilty of seven out of eight indictments after winning himself a not-proven verdict on the Anne Knielands charge. He wasn't charged with a Newcastle taxi driver's murder either, despite the fact that the police had attributed the killing to him.

Manuel was sentenced to death and hanged at Barlinnie Prison on 11 July 1958. It was reported by the prison officers who led Manuel to his doom that he showed no fear and almost trotted towards the gallows room as if looking forward to what was about to happen to him.

While waiting for the hangman, he admitted to three other murders: Helen Carlin, a prostitute from Pimlico, London; Anne Steel in Glasgow in 1956; and Ellen Petrie, who he stabbed to death in June 1956. In total, he is thought to have murdered fifteen people, all of them strangers.

This beast wasn't a gangster; he was someone who killed for the sake of killing. He had no connections with any of his victims. He blasted people to death inside their homes: no one was safe – men, girls and a boy. He was a real loner who loved the dark and who lived with his parents in Birkenshaw, the centre of his killing territory.

What makes a man want to kill indiscriminately? Just as had been the case with Thomas Hamilton at Dunblane, where he had barely known any of his victims, so it was with Manuel. Just like it took Hamilton's death to bring it all to an end, so it was with Manuel. Scotland sleeps cautiously with these men in mind...

Chillingly, Manuel took police to the spot where he had buried seventeen-year-old Isabella Cooke; it was a scene reminiscent of when Ian Brady took police to Saddleworth Moor in Yorkshire, when he and Hindley were flown there by helicopter to walk on the graves of their victims.

When Manuel took authorities to the spot, he told them: 'This is the place. In fact, I think I'm standing on her now.'

In a bizarre twist, after Manuel had been released from one of his prison sentences in 1957, he visited Newcastle-upon-Tyne, where he hired a taxi. The driver was Sydney Dunn. The following day, a policeman cycling along a moorland road near Edmundbyers, some twenty miles from Newcastle, found the car abandoned. There were signs of fresh blood on the seats. A search for the driver was soon underway and, within hours, police discovered the body of Sydney Dunn... his throat had been slashed and he had been shot.

The downfall of Peter Manuel came about when he started to flash his cash about: wrong for a man who was normally broke. The police managed to recover some of the £1 notes that Manuel had been passing around. They were from a newly-printed batch and, when the serial numbers were checked, it was discovered that they had been paid over to one of his victims, Peter Smart, who had cashed a cheque in preparation to go on holiday.

Police arrested Manuel and placed him in an ID parade. Staff and drinkers at a bar identified him as being the man who had handed over the new blue notes; the ones that were in the same sequence as the notes that had been given to Peter Smart.

Manuel goes down as one of the most callous killers in Scottish criminal history.

THOMAS WEST HAMILTON

On the morning of Wednesday, 13 March 1996, Thomas West Hamilton shattered the peaceful country town of

Dunblane, Stirlingshire, with a fusillade of gunfire that sent shockwaves around not just Scotland but the world.

Allegedly armed with four handguns, Hamilton entered the gym room of a quiet primary school in Dunblane and began firing at a class of five- to six-year-old children. Sixteen of the children died in the violent outrage, as well as their teacher, Gwen Mayor, who was shot as she tried in vain to protect them.

The investigation that followed showed that Hamilton had become increasingly unbalanced because he believed that people in authority were constantly persecuting him. He had been forced to leave his position in the Boy Scouts and blamed the Scouting Association for ruining his life. He started up several 'youth movements' himself, but parents became increasingly worried about his behaviour and withdrew their children from them.

Hamilton thought that a conspiracy was being waged against him and even wrote to the Queen to complain. Finally, he slipped over the edge into insanity and perpetrated the dreadful slaughter in Dunblane.

Thomas Hamilton has been attributed with murdering seventeen innocent people. There are three versions to what happened: the media version, the covered-up version and the truth. Now, one of the amazing things about being behind bars is the information you get hold of. I mean, why are the police always sniffing around prisons? Because they know that it is the men already behind bars who so often hold the keys to their crime puzzles.

The fascinating and terrifying things I have discovered about this man in the last few years are nobody's business. Well... until now. What I have uncovered is both fascinating and terrifying at the same time; it has fundamentally altered the ideas I held about society. When I started out on this journey, I could never have envisaged how the authorities' force of denial could have reached out so far.

There is no doubt that Hamilton was a cunning, evil bastard. The 1989 Children Act says that only clubs for under-eights require leaders to be checked out in advance by local councils to see if they are 'fit persons'. To overcome this, Hamilton began recruiting over-eights. He always kept himself within the law and, obviously, someone was advising him how to do that.

The British government has covered up the truth by granting bereaved parents their dearest wish – a ban on handguns. However, the handgun ban has done little to reduce gun deaths. On the other hand, possibly as a result of what happened at Dunblane, there have been copycat massacres in Port Arthur in Tasmania and in Columbine in the USA.

The underworld consensus of opinion is that the Dunblane murderer's plan did not actually involve the premeditated killing of children. Hamilton's plan was to kill the head teacher; it was only when this plan was foiled that he embarked on his random rampage.

It was a plan that went horribly wrong and when things go wrong, the worst can happen. Hamilton's original plans were scuppered. Another example of this came in the Hungerford massacre. Michael Ryan killed a woman when she fought off his attempts to rape her. Once he had killed her, it triggered off a whole chain of events and a full-scale massacre ensued. This is similar to what I believe happened at Dunblane.

Given that Thomas Hamilton had just murdered sixteen children and their teacher, as well as attempting to murder at least fifteen others, it might not seem significant for me to tell you that Hamilton may have been murdered himself.

The legal establishment portrayed his death as suicide, but why would they have wanted to have it that way?

What was it that caused Thomas Hamilton, a perverted character, to enter that school on that day and shoot those children? The public inquiry, headed by Lord Cullen in the summer of 1996, was not a criminal prosecution, merely an attempt to ensure that justice was being seen to be done.

At the inquest, a varied selection of Thomas Hamilton's friends were desperate to tell us what a boring man he was; there were also some extremely insignificant witnesses who testified that train tickets had been bought, as well as some vital witnesses, such as the staff of Dunblane Primary School who had been caught up in this horrific tragic incident.

However, it was not the witnesses who were present at the inquiry that aroused my interest; it was those who were not called to attend. In particular, there was an off-duty policeman who had been the first person on the scene – to this day, nobody knows who he is.

In 1999, it was discovered that the Crown had slapped a 100-year closure order on the gathered evidence. The excuse given was to protect the identities of the children who Hamilton had come into contact with over the years. This is rubbish: the names could have simply been blanked out, as had been the case in the Bichard Inquiry that took place after the Soham murders. The Scottish Record Office proposed the Dunblane closure and other documents were also subject to the 100-year closure. How can they justify claiming that the closure was intended only to protect the identity of children? It is ridiculous to suggest that each and every one of these pages contains the name of a child.

Another thing: why was an unstable character such as Thomas Hamilton allowed to possess a firearms certificate in the first place? Press reports after the shooting considered him to be an unstable character, one that was not suited to hold such a certificate. There was also, it is believed, a police report confirming this.

Lord Cullen stated that, prior to the shooting, there was no evidence of criminal behaviour on the part of Thomas Hamilton. Who are the children named in the productions? What can be so sensitive that it cannot be made public for 100 years?

The witnesses who were not called to the inquiry could have provided crucial evidence. It is known that a police officer had been in the school at the time of, or shortly after, the shooting. He, it is claimed, advised the first ambulance crew to arrive, saying that it was safe to enter the gym as Hamilton was dead.

On a matter as serious as this, a police officer would have confirmed the facts himself before advising the ambulance crew, so the police officer in question had definitely been in the gym. Here we have an officer who had been present at the scene, someone who had been trained to observe and to give evidence, so why was he not called to give evidence at the inquiry? How come an injured schoolboy is alleged to have said that he saw the 'bad man' (Thomas Hamilton) being shot by a policeman? There are serious doubts as to how Thomas Hamilton died. The gun that it is claimed he used to kill himself would have just about blown his head right off. Yet a teacher claimed that he thought he saw Hamilton's body moving after the fatal shot. On seeing Hamilton's body, the senior ambulance officer remarked that he had wanted to kick it – even though Hamilton's head had probably been blown off?

Why was Hamilton's body removed from the scene so speedily and why was it cremated so soon after the massacre? It clouds the events of the last few minutes of his life. The authorities have complicated matters further by attempting to have part of Thomas Hamilton's autopsy report hidden for – you've guessed it – 100 years.

Thomas Hamilton had some very dubious associates, yet no serious attempts were made to discover what had driven Hamilton to commit such a crime. It could have started with something as simple as a small lie to protect the identity of someone in the public eye who had, at one time, known Thomas Hamilton but who now did not wish that innocent acquaintanceship to become public knowledge. On the other hand, there could have

Above left: Arthur Thompson: safecracker, robber, protection racketeer and illegal bookmaker, he was blown up, shot and run over by rivals, to no avail.

Above right: Paddy Meehan, serial safecracker and escaper who travelled to East Germany to seek asylum.

Below left: Arthur 'Fatty' Thompson Junior, successor to the family 'trade', shot dead.

Below right: Paul Ferris, once best friend of Arthur Jr, was acquitted of his shooting after the longest trial in Scottish legal history.

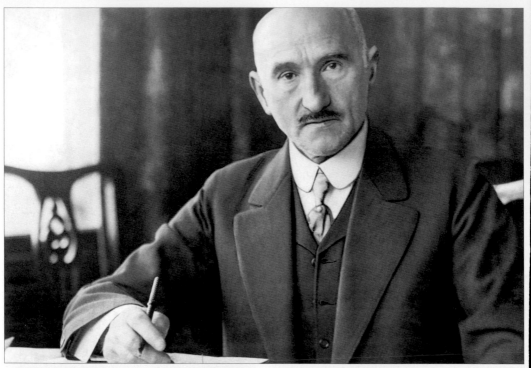

Above: Oscar Slater was imprisoned in the granite walls of Peterhead for 19 years before his conviction for murder was quashed on appeal.

Below left: Johnny Ramensky, first man to escape successfully from Peterhead, was a demolition expert recruited by the army to blow up Goering's safe.

Below right: On the day he died, Griffiths had shot a total of fourteen innocent people before he was himself killed by police gunfire.

Left: William 'Tank' McGuiness, a well-known and extremely violent Glaswegian, confessed to a murder of which Meehan had already been convicted.

Right: Jimmy Boyle, a colourful character in Scottish criminal history.

Left: Walter Scott Ellis, aka the arch criminal 'Watty', was part of the infamous Hole in the Wall gang that was responsible for a string of armed robberies.

Above: Frank McPhee murdered a man at his friend's wedding and then went on to cause a war with other heavy gangsters.

Above right and right: James Crosbie, the record-breaking serial bankrobber and now talented writer.

20 YEARS IN JAIL FOR BANK ROBBER ON A BIKE

By ARNOT McWHINNIE

PRISONER WITH A SECRET

Most of the money which Crosbie and his accomplice stole is still missing.

TRAINEE pilot James Crosbie CYCLED from Scotland's biggest-ever bank robbery with his £87,000 haul in a rucksack.

Yesterday, the bank raider with a passion for high flying and big spending WALKED from the High Court to a 20-year jail sentence.

The court, in Edinburgh, had heard how Crosbie, 37, pulled off three armed bank hold-ups which netted £170,150.

Although he pleaded guilty, Crosbie has remained tight-lipped about what happened to the bulk of the stolen cash. Almost £115,000 has vanished.

Earlier, Mr James Milligan, QC, prosecuting, outlined the remarkable series of robberies.

£65,704 from the Clydesdale Bank branch at Queen Elizabeth Avenue, Hillington, Renfrewshire, on May 23, 1972.

£87,000 from the Clydesdale branch at 1050 Dumbarton Road, W. iteinch, Glasgow, on April 30 this year— Scotland's biggest raid.

And £17,446 from the Royal Bank of Scotland branch at 8 Gorgie

Brian Cockerill, 'The Taxman'. A true hard bastard.

Above left: Peter Manuel, one of the most callous killers in Scottish criminal history and the last man to be hanged in Glasgow.

Above right: A monster of the Scottish penal system, Dennis Nilsen needs no introduction.

Below left: Ian Brady and Myra Hindley, the Moors Murderers.

Below right: Who was – or is – the multiple murderer Bible John? The case remains unsolved…

Left: Big Mags Haney – vociferous anti-paedophile campaigner, granny and convicted drug-dealer.

Above: Joe Steele knows how to publicise a cause

Left: On the roof at Peterhead.

Above: In an audacious escape attempt with Joe Steele, bankrobber John Croll dressed as a prison warden to walk out of Perth Prison.

Below: Roadblocks were set up to catch hard bastard Tommy Gordon, who escaped from Peterhead. Eventually he was recaptured down south.

been a paedophile ring in operation – that would have been much more serious.

Take a closer look at Thomas Hamilton and the people with whom he was connected who were involved in his paedophilic activities. Hamilton loved the power and control his guns gave him and it probably did not occur to him that he could be killed with a gun just as easily as he had killed others with a gun. Six-year-old Matthew Birnie, who was injured in the incident, said from his hospital bed a few days later: 'I know the bad man is dead because the policeman shot him.' Eleven-year-old Laura Bryce, listening to what was happening that morning from Hut 7, said that she had heard a man scream and guessed that this must have been the moment when Hamilton shot himself. It is hard to believe that Hamilton screamed when he put the gun in his mouth. It is much more likely that he screamed when his assassin put a gun in his mouth.

Hamilton had set out to kill Ron Taylor, the head teacher of Dunblane Primary School. He had planned to do this in front of morning assembly, in particular, in front of the Primary 7 boys. It was going to be an eye-for-an-eye killing. In Hamilton's eyes, Taylor had humiliated him by warning the boys in assembly to have nothing to do with him. He was out for revenge, but his plan was foiled. As a consequence, the massacre happened.

Then, when a few agitators started asking questions about the legality of hiding information away, we were told that it was to protect the child victims of Hamilton's abuse. It is only natural and right that we should be confused.

The boys Hamilton abused are now young men. Even at the time of the Cullen Inquiry, in 1996, many of them would have been in their late teens. It should have been their choice whether they gave evidence or not. The boys at the 1988 camp on Inchmoan Island in particular must surely be traumatised by their ordeal. Doreen Hagger, who helped out at the camp, had to leave the island in the middle of the night for her own personal safety and to get help for these boys. The distress and guilt she felt at having to leave them behind, when they pleaded with her to take them with her, must still live with her today.

Make no mistake, but this – the long years of Thomas Hamilton's reign, the Dunblane tragedy, the aftermath, the Cullen Inquiry, the hidden documents – this, is Scotland's shame.

Even before the inquiry began, the bereaved and injured children's parents were not advised about having legal representation. One parent said: 'It wasn't made clear to us until some time after the events had taken place that the parents would require legal representation. I feel that this should have been brought to the attention of the parents the moment they were informed of the tragic circumstances. It was mainly by accident that my husband and I became aware that we did require, like other parents, to be legally represented.'

Hamilton lied about his qualifications so that he could meet the requirements of the regional council. He was the holder of a Women's Assistant Coach Award, Class 5, which would qualify him to assist in the teaching of women's artistic gymnastics while under the supervision of a Class 4 coach or above. Qualified assistant coaches may work under the direction of a qualified coach, but they must not work unsupervised.

I believe that Hamilton had been part of a very active paedophile ring. If so, where are the other men now? Who are they? What are they doing? Have they given up their paedophilic activities since March 1996?

Hamilton used to run summer camps for children, and one particular camp was on Inchmoan Island in July and August 1988. It was planned that children would reside on the island for blocks of one week, Sunday to Sunday, for up to a maximum of six weeks. No parental visits were allowed and phone calls by children to their parents were at Hamilton's discretion. During this camp, a number of incidents were alleged to have taken place whereby Hamilton assaulted children as punishment for misbehaviour or because they had failed to perform exercises to his expectation.

Following one incident, on 17 July 1988, the police were called and found thirteen children wearing swimming trunks and one supervisor... Hamilton. At 9.00pm a complaint was made to the police regarding assaults on and lack of supervision for the children attending the island. On arriving at the scene, officers from Central Scotland Police found the campsite on the east shore and a group of eight-year-old boys playing, unsupervised.

Of the thirteen children there, only three stated they were enjoying themselves; the remainder stated that they were homesick, unable to contact their parents, that the food they were provided with was poor and that Hamilton was too strict.

On 21 July, the children were taken ashore by the police. Their parents were contacted and informed of the circumstances in which the children had been found. The children were then taken to Dumbarton Police Office; parents took several of them home, but some were returned to Hamilton's care.

At a secret boot camp, that Hamilton called his Sea Rovers Patrol, he trained boys to kill using live ammo. At night, sick Hamilton would make them assume the press-up position, would then whip them with a steel rod and rub lotion onto their wounds. Sick or what? Hamilton would also take many hundreds of photographs of young boys wearing tightly-fitting swimming trunks. What did he do with them? Where are these photographs now?

One angry parent confronted Hamilton and demanded that he hand over the photographs he had taken of his son. Hamilton, of course, only handed over the ones that he wanted to hand over. Hamilton was passing these photographs onto a paedophile ring... a paedophile ring that wanted him dead. That is why he was allowed to go on his killing spree, so that he could be snuffed out. He was a loose cannon who knew too much about his perverted associates.

The top and bottom of it is that this sick bastard walked into a primary school and pulled out an arsenal of guns. The teachers, so they say, didn't know what was going on. Even more harrowing, the little five-year-old angels must have thought that it was a movie, until this monster started emptying his high-powered handguns into them. However, there is a 'missing' half hour in Hamilton's morning itinerary – from his leaving home that morning to his arrival at Dunblane School – that cannot be accounted for.

He carried on running around the school shooting every little child he saw. After he shot and killed a full class of five-year-olds, he turned his guns on the teacher who tried to reason with him. Nothing would make him stop.

However, as I have already hinted at, there is one big question to consider. The ambulancewoman, Alison Irvine (non-witness), states that when she and her colleague Leslie Haire arrived at the school at 9.57am there were no police cars and no uniformed police officers in attendance – just a man who described himself as an 'off-duty police officer' (in his evidence, Ron Taylor also refers to an 'off-duty police officer' being present on the scene).

Ron Taylor met the ambulance crew at the door of the school and told them that they were the first people on the scene. Les Haire went back to the ambulance to radio up that it was a major incident, while Mr Taylor led Alison Irvine to the gym. The 'off-duty police officer' told her that it was safe to go in. He reassured her that the gunman – Hamilton – was dead. So we have a mysterious Mr X, someone who all and sundry knew to be an off-duty police officer... how did they know that he was the person he claimed to be?

It was stated that Hamilton's body was almost against

the top wall. His head was facing towards the top wall. If he had shot himself facing the wall, he would have been thrown backwards. His feet would have been touching the top wall, not his head.

It has always been claimed that Hamilton intended to shoot all the children in the school, over 700 of them. A bag was found near to his body in the gym, yet Hamilton was not seen entering the school carrying such a bag. Was the bag containing the additional ammunition placed there to justify his killing, if such facts ever came to light? That way it could be claimed that whoever shot Hamilton had successfully limited the scale of the massacre.

One couple, whose child was in the gym that day, but who was uninjured, said that upon visiting the gym afterwards, they saw two bullet holes at the top end of the gym, where they were told that Hamilton had killed himself. They state that there were no other bullet holes in the wall. These two bullet holes were six inches from the floor and approximately two inches apart. So, Hamilton shot himself twice through the head, just like the Deepcut Barracks soldiers did, eh?

Why was the pathologist repeatedly warned by the Lord Advocate to refer only to Hamilton's head injury and not to other areas of his body? Hadn't Hamilton, supposedly, shot himself in the head? I believe that Hamilton was shot in the torso and that he was then finished off – in the head – by some unknown person. The evidence given refers to a gunshot wound to the stomach and hip and two gunshot wounds to the head, via the mouth. Four shots! Hamilton was a well-known coward who likely didn't have it in him to shoot himself. A scream was heard coming from the gym: perhaps Hamilton screaming for his life. His killer then exited from the gym fire door.

Why was Hamilton's dead body moved around in the school gym? Oh yes, his body had been moved, something that was confirmed by someone present at the scene. Was it the 'off-duty policeman'? If so, why?

Hamilton must have known that he wouldn't have been safe in prison; even the other sex cases would have turned on him. This dirty monster is Scotland's worst-ever child killer. So, as far as I'm concerned, I have no problem with the fact that he was probably murdered.

DENNIS NILSEN

Dennis Nilsen, who killed fifteen men, came from a little place in the northeast of Scotland called Fraserburg, a place best known as a fishing port. Nilsen's mother and relatives still live in the area.

In early evening, February 1983, a Dyno-rod employee called Michael Cattran was sent to investigate the cause of a blockage in the drains at 23 Cranley Gardens, Muswell Hill. He found a strange substance in the sewer, which he later explained to his boss he thought was human flesh. It had flowed from a pipe leading to flat A.

Since it was too dark to do anything that evening, Cattran returned to the scene the following morning with his boss. On their return, the substance had disappeared. One of the occupants of the flats told them that they thought that the man who resided in the attic flat had made a visit to the manhole during the course of the night. The police were called immediately.

Although the substance had been removed, Cattran somehow had been able to salvage some pieces of flesh and four small bones from the waste pipe of number 23. These were handed over to Detective Chief Inspector Peter Jay, who immediately had them examined by an expert: the flesh and the bones were confirmed to be of human origin.

The occupant of the attic flat had gone to work when Detective Chief Inspector Jay, Detective Inspector McCusker and Detective Butler attended the premises. They decided to await his return. The owner of the attic flat was a thirty-eight-year-old Scottish bachelor employed as a Civil Service clerk. He was a former trainee butcher and had once been a probationary policeman. His name was Dennis Andrew Nilsen. He was told about the discovery of the human remains in the drains and expressed suitable horror. Jay told him bluntly to stop wasting everyone's time and to tell them where the rest of the body could be found: 'In two plastic bags in the wardrobe next door,' said Nilsen. 'I'll show you.'

Nilsen was then removed and taken to Hornsey police station. During transit, McCusker asked Nilsen: 'Are you talking about one or two bodies?' 'Fifteen or sixteen,' came the reply. Nilsen had murdered a dozen or more young men at his previous address of 195 Melrose Avenue and three at his residence at 23a Cranley Gardens.

Few of the victims had been missed, as they had been from the underbelly of London's homeless and unemployed. These young men had each been drawn into Nilsen's home.

When the wardrobes were checked, body parts were found in black bags. Some of the parts were in an advanced stage of decomposition. In the bathroom, the legs of his last victim, Stephen Sinclair, were found. A tea chest in the flat held more body parts. Carrier bags held three heads. All of the parts were taken to a mortuary and were assembled to form three incomplete corpses.

Nilsen had left the remains of twelve earlier victims at Melrose Avenue in Cricklewood. He used to store the bodies under the floorboards in his ground-floor flat. When he found that he could only store a limited amount, he would remove an old one and replace it with a new body. The old bodies could be up to a year old, before they were dismembered, packed into a suitcase and stored in his garden shed. After the number of suitcases had started to pile up, he began burning his victims' remains, together with their clothing. He would burn tyres with the bodies to hide the horrific stench of burning flesh. Once the fire had burnt out, he would smash the bones into small pieces with a spade.

Nilsen explained how he had once had a bad fright at Melrose Avenue. A man he was trying to strangle had fought back and escaped. The police were called and an inspector and a sergeant had questioned him as he stood on the floorboards that covered the remains of five previous victims. Always articulate, Nilsen managed to convince the police that it had been nothing more than a homosexual lovers' tiff.

The owners of Melrose Avenue decided to sell the property. Nilsen quickly cut up and burned all of the bodies from under the floorboards. He then moved on to Cranley Gardens, where he did not have access to the garden, so he decided to boil the body parts and then flush them down the toilet. The larger bones were either disposed of in the rubbish bin or on wasteland at the rear of the property.

One of the victims was a semi-vagrant called John Howlett. They had been drinking in a public house after having met in an off-license. They then went back to Nilsen's home, had a meal and sat watching television, where they consumed more alcohol.

Nilsen then asked Howlett to leave. He refused, and Nilsen tried to strangle him with a strap. The man fought back; they struggled on the bed and Howlett went limp – blood from a wound on Howlett's head soaked the bedding. Howlett then started to breathe again, so Nilsen tried to strangle him once more. He dragged the unconscious Howlett to the bathroom, placed him in the bath and filled it with water. Bubbles flowed from Howlett's nose to the surface of the water, which now contained blood, food and other bodily emissions.

When asked by his solicitor why he had killed these young men, Nilsen replied: 'I am hoping you will tell me that.' The nearest anyone could come to an explanation was that Nilsen was a lonely man who felt isolated. It is believed that he had killed his victims to ensure that they never left him.

There was never any doubt about Nilsen's guilt. He

admitted to his crimes on many occasions and talked about them both freely and openly. The difficulty came in deciding whether Nilsen was downright evil or insane, as was often the case with people who pleaded insanity – it was the same at the trial of the Yorkshire Ripper.

Nilsen was interviewed over a period of thirty days, producing 157 pages of evidence. He said that between 1978 and 1983, he had strangled young men. It became clear that Nilsen had invited other young men to his home, but they had left unharmed. 'Each of the murdered had been in near-helpless intoxication,' Nilsen said, before he went on to strangle them with a tie.

Dennis Nilsen was convicted and sentenced to life imprisonment. He apparently accepted his punishment and does not expect to be released. He is Scotland's second-worst serial killer. In early 2005, Nilsen was interviewed in prison by police and admitted to another killing, which he said was his first, after he was shown a grainy photograph of missing fourteen-year-old Stephen Holmes, the son of Irish emigrants, who disappeared in London in December 1978. In 2005, the English prison service put a block on Nilsen publishing a trilogy of books relating to his life. In a court ruling, Nilsen lost his fight to have one of the manuscripts released from prison service possession; another script is with Nilsen's solicitor and cannot be sent back to Nilsen for fear of it being seized by the authorities. Currently Nilsen transcribes books into Braille, using high-tech computer programmes for twenty hours a week.

IAN BRADY

Moors murderer Ian Brady was born Ian Duncan Stewart on 2 January 1938 in Glasgow, Scotland. He is responsible for a series of murders that took place between 1962 and 1965 in Greater Manchester. Brady and Myra Hindley met in 1961: she was a nineteen-year-old typist; he was a twenty-three-year-old stock clerk. By 1966, both were tried at Chester Assizes for multiple murders: the trial lasted fifteen days and, on 6 May 1966, they were both sentenced to life imprisonment.

Brady and Hindley worked in the same office. After hours, they developed a violent appetite for sadism, Nazism and pornography. In September 1964, the couple went to live with Hindley's grandmother in Hattersley, Yorkshire. They were also friendly with Hindley's sister Maureen and her husband, seventeen-year-old David Smith. With his books on sadism and handguns, Brady sought to impress Smith. Between them they talked of robbing banks and, even worse, of murder.

Not wishing to look like an idle boaster, Brady picked up seventeen-year-old Edward Evans, a homosexual, in Manchester on the evening of 6 October 1965 and took him home. Later that night, at 11.30pm, Hindley went to Smith's house and asked him to come home with her. Smith was going to be shown a murder.

When he returned, Smith found a young man on the sofa in the living room. He was still alive, but Brady, wielding an axe, proceeded to smash his head in. He said: 'It's done. It's the messiest yet. It normally only takes one blow.'

Smith was terrified by what he had seen and, early the next morning, he telephoned the police telling them that he had just witnessed a murder and that he was convinced that others had been committed.

On 7 October 1965, at approximately 7.30am, police officers descended on 16 Wardle Brook Avenue, Manchester. On arriving at the street, a police officer noticed a bread man at the end of the street and asked if he could borrow his uniform. The police officer then posed as the bread man, and knocked on the door of 16 Wardle Brook Avenue and Myra Hindley answered the door. Once inside the house, they saw a man sleeping in the lounge wearing his underclothes – Ian Brady.

They were told why the police officers where at their home. The police then went upstairs and tried one of the bedroom doors, which was locked. Myra said that it was where she kept her firearms and that the keys were unavailable. An officer told her that the door could very easily be forced open, at which point Brady, no doubt realising that the police officers weren't going to go away, said to Hindley: 'You'd better give him the keys.'

Talbot and another police officer went upstairs, opened the bedroom door and found the body of Edward Evans, trussed up in the foetal position in a clear plastic bag. No one at this stage could have realised the horror that was about to unravel.

A further search produced two left-luggage tickets that corresponded to two suitcases at Manchester Central Station. The police found the cases and, inside them, chanced upon one of the most revealing discoveries;

revelations that would haunt them for the rest of their lives. Among the coshes, wigs, papers and photographs were two tape recordings. Some of the photographs were of a little girl – ten-year-old Lesley Ann Downey, who had been missing from her home since December 1964.

The child's screaming voice was identified on a tape recording pleading to be allowed to go home. The tape went on to a reveal the girl's heart-rending cries of pain as she was brutality tortured with pliers. Commands were heard from Brady telling her what to do. When they had finished with her, they killed her. Her body was later discovered on Oldham moors, north of Manchester.

Another child, twelve-year-old John Kilbride, who had been missing from home since November 1963, featured in some of Brady's notes – notes which were a plan of murder. From photographs showing Brady and Hindley on the moors, police were able to identify search areas. John Kilbride's moorland grave was found a few hundred yards away from that of Lesley Ann Downey.

The Moors Murderers continued to excite interest in the 1980s and 1990s, first with suggestions that Hindley had become a socially reformed character who was fit to be paroled and, secondly, by persistent rumours that there were more bodies to be found on the moors. Despite a strong campaign on her behalf by the late Lord Longford, Hindley remained in prison until her death in 2002. Brady, who is detained in Park Lane High Security Hospital, Liverpool, has said that he never wants to be released. Having gone on various hunger strikes, wanting to die, he seems to have survived for quite some time.

A private confession in 1986 by Hindley to two more killings led to searches on Saddleworth Moor for further graves. Her confession was made public in April 1987 and it became known that she and Brady admitted killing Keith Bennett, aged 12, and Pauline Reade, aged 16. Some twenty-four years after the girl had been murdered, her body was found in August 1987. At different times both Hindley and Brady assisted the police in their searches by being taking to the moors in a helicopter.

In January 1988, the Director of Public Prosecutions announced that no further charges would be brought against the Moors Murderers. Since then, Brady has written a manuscript – relating to the murders – that he has given to his solicitor. He has asked for the manuscript to be sold to a publisher in the event of his death.

Brady courted more controversy when he wrote a book on serial killers. Despite the fact that he didn't mention his own crimes, it caused a public outcry. However, it still sold well and his royalty cheques went to his elderly mother.

Hindley, her body ravaged by the effects of chain smoking, eventually made it out of prison... in a wooden box.

Ian Brady and Myra Hindley killed for kicks. They developed a sick, mutual thrill from killing innocent children. Brady was well on the way to being a full-blown psychopath. He had a private library of books about torture and ritual killing, his favourite being the works of the infamous Marquis de Sade.

Hindley was quickly influenced and dominated by her

older boyfriend, whom she regarded as an intellectual genius – as did Brady himself. She soon took an avid interest in his books on leather fetishism, sexual sadism and bondage, at a time when pornography was outlawed in a far stricter fashion that it is today.

Brady also had a fascination with Hitler, something he shared with many other famous psychopaths. Nazi brutality seems to appeal to people that have a sense of wanting to grasp power by any method they can. Apart from idolising Hitler, Brady had a favourite movie that he and Hindley would watch time and time again... the *Nuremberg War Trials*.

Detective Inspector Stan Egerton referred to the area where Hindley had been brought up as the 'slumps'; an area where the houses were two-up, two-down with no baths and an outside toilet. The good thing about the area was that everyone knew everyone and knew what he or she was up to. If a stranger arrived on the scene everyone would know about it. Myra had a happy childhood, but with very little money – a common theme in that particular neighbourhood.

Brady, on the other hand, had endured a tough childhood. He was the son of a waitress who came from Glasgow and did not know who his father was. It has been stated that, as he grew up, he was different to other children of the same age: instead of listening to rock 'n' roll music he preferred classical music and read classical books. He also dressed differently in an attempt to stand out from the other youngsters.

Stan Egerton said that Brady was an oddball and a

loner. Jean Ritchie, the author of a biography on Myra Hindley, said that Brady had fantasies about killing, but that he would probably not have carried them out if he had not met Hindley. They gelled together and formed a stronger, more brutal, force than they would have had separately.

ROBERT BLACK

Robert Black was born in the Highland village of Kinlochleven in Argyleshire and even as a young schoolboy displayed all the signs of wickedness. He had always been a bully and was disliked by the other children, who called him 'Beasty' and 'Smelly' on account of his very strong body odour. As a result, Black grew up an outcast and, according to some criminal psychologists, turned on young girls to revenge his past rejection when he reached adulthood.

Unless Black confesses, no one will ever know for certain how many young girls died at his hands. A van driver, he travelled the length and breadth of Britain, taking every opportunity he could to snatch girls and sexually abuse them before killing and dumping their bodies far away from the place of their abduction.

It is known that he killed Susan Maxwell (aged 11), Caroline Hogg (aged 5) and Sarah Harper (aged 10), and that he was already serving life for the kidnapping and sexual assault of a six-year-old girl when he was sentenced to ten life sentences at Newcastle Crown Court on 4 May 1994.

He is suspected of having killed at least thirteen other

young girls in Britain, and police think it is entirely possible that he carried out his perverted attacks and killings on young girls on the continent.

As he was leaving the dock, after receiving his ten life sentences, he turned to the seated policemen and sneered: 'Well done, boys.'

No one knows how many perverts like Black are lurking about in our cities, towns and villages, but it is hoped that some mistake will expose them and reveal the depths of their depravity. Black is currently serving his life sentence in Wakefield Prison (known as Monster Mansion) in England, where he will spend the rest of his natural life.

When Caroline Hogg went missing in Edinburgh, there was a massive British hunt for her but, sadly, the little girl was never found alive. I can remember the events clearly, as I was in Carluke children's home at the time when this monster also snatched Susan Maxwell, the little girl who was doing her paper round. I do know that Interpol has interviewed Black for murders all over Europe: he may be one of the most prolific serial killers that Britain, not just Scotland, has ever seen.

BIBLE JOHN?

The City of Glasgow Police has a question mark after the name 'Bible John'. For although they know he murdered three young women in the late 1960s, after picking them up in Glasgow's famous Barrowland Ballroom, and even though they had an eyewitness, they have never been able to identify the man they call Bible John.

The first murder took place on 23 February 1968, when nurse Pat Docker went dancing at the Barrowland Ballroom. She was found beaten up and strangled with her own tights.

Efforts were made to trace her movements after she left the dance hall. Taxi drivers were questioned and a thousand posters showing her picture and asking for help were distributed, all to no avail. No one came forward and no progress was made towards the solving of the brutal murder.

The next murder occurred on 17 August 1969. On the evening of Saturday 16 August, Jemima McDonald visited the Barrowland, where she was seen in the company of a tall, smartly dressed man with reddish-fair hair that was cut unfashionably short. Thirty hours later Jemima's body was found, battered and with her tights pulled tightly around her neck. Police again failed to make any progress in solving the murder.

With the third and (as far as we know) last victim, the police became confident that they would catch the killer: they now had an eyewitness who had spoken to the man.

On the night of 30 October, Helen Puttock went to Barrowland with her sister Jeannie. There she met and danced with a man who had introduced himself as John. At the end of the evening both girls and 'John' shared a taxi, dropping Jeannie off first before carrying on to Helen's home.

The next morning a man out walking his dog discovered Helen's naked body in a lane. She had been badly beaten about the head and strangled with her own tights.

A shocked Jeannie was able to give the police a description of the man who had escorted them home, mentioning also that he had a biblical turn of phrase; hence the sobriquet – Bible John.

A distinctive identikit photo was produced and widely circulated, and for months, even years afterwards, anyone remotely resembling the picture was questioned and eliminated. Despite this, the police drew no closer to their quarry and Bible John remained anonymous. It was even suspected that a policeman or a serviceman could be responsible for the murders. The height, unfashionably short hair, neat appearance and articulacy made this a distinct possibility.

Detective Superintendent Joe Beattie, the man in charge of the investigation, committed hundred of officers to the hunt and the case has never been closed. As late as February 1996 the body of a suspect, who had been buried for over sixteen years, was exhumed and his remains tested for DNA evidence, but still no positive results were forthcoming. The file will never be closed on this evil monster.

GAVIN McGUIRE

Gavin McGuire walked free from prison after serving ten years for sexually assaulting and attempting to murder an innocent twenty-three-year-old woman. Three months after his release, he followed Mhairi Julyan, a teenage schoolgirl who was making her way home from a pantomime. She was with her friends and, once she was near her home, she bade her friends goodnight and set off on the short trip to her parents' house.

She never made it. The sexual predator McGuire grabbed her from behind and the girl never stood a chance: the monster is over 6ft tall and weighs some 17st. He dragged the poor girl to the bus station in Kilmarnock, where he raped her and then murdered her. He then cut off poor Mhairi's head and dumped it in a nearby garden. I don't know whether he was trying to throw her head into a bin and missed, but how could any normal human do such a monstrous thing to a pretty little girl?

When I was in the Peterhead special unit, I was involved in an armed siege with my friend Stewart Gillespie. We were removed from the unit over to the main part of the prison, where we were held until the prison could get hold of the Cat A van to take Stewart and I back to the seg blocks in Shotts and Barlinnie. I was placed next door to the monster McGuire.

He tapped the pipe that runs through all the cells and asked who I was. I knew he was a sex case because the hall I had been placed in was full of them. He told me that his name was Gavin McGuire and that he was the prison's top man. I burst out laughing and told him that I would cut his fucking throat if he ever came into normal mainstream prison. He got a twenty-five-year recommendation.

`HONEYMONSTER´

'Honeymonster' comes from Port Glasgow. He was the first animal I came across in Glenochil back in 1991.

It all started when the Honeymonster befriended his neighbour. The woman could have only felt sorry him, as this animal really does look like the Honeymonster from the Sugar Puffs TV advert.

Once he managed to get into the woman's flat, he strangled her with his bare hands, then stripped and raped her repeatedly. However, even this did not quench this monster's thirst. He took her back into his own smelly flat and hid her in his wardrobe. Eventually the woman's mother came calling on her daughter.

When there was no answer, she tapped on his door to see if he had seen her daughter. He told her that he hadn't seen her for some time, but the woman knew he was lying – she could also smell the rotten stench coming from his flat. Suspicious, she went to the police and told them what she had seen... and smelled. The police got a search warrant.

When they entered the Honeymonster's flat, they found the woman's daughter's decomposed, naked body lying in his cupboard. The monster broke down and confessed to the police that he had murdered her and told them that he was sorry. He has since been battered, scalded and coshed in Glenochil Prison.

The SPS managed to get him to a specialist to buffer the hump from his back. I kid you not, this monster didn't deserve to get any special treatment, but he told the shrinks that he had only committed these animalistic, sickening offences, against this pretty woman who had shown him some kindness, because he looked like a freak.

WILLIAM BEGGS

The 'Limbs in the Loch' case saw William Beggs, then aged thirty-eight, being branded the 'Gay Ripper' when, in October 2001, he was caged for at least twenty years for the animalistic murder, butchering and then dumping of the body of eighteen-year-old Ayrshire shop worker Barry Wallace.

The Edinburgh High Court judge, Lord Osborne, told the Ulster-born Beggs from Portadown, County Armagh, not to expect to be released on parole at the end of the twenty years. Police were lining up to quiz Beggs about a string of unsolved murders.

So distressing was the nature of the evidence that that the trial judge took the unusual step of exempting the trial jury from further service for the next ten years. The gruesome evidence included how Beggs had used a saw and knife to cut up his teenage victim's limbs and body – even snapping some of his bones in two with his hands.

Before carrying out his evil act of butchery, he handcuffed his victim, injured him and then sexually assaulted him. Afterwards, he weighed the limbs and torso down with bricks and dumped then in Loch Lomond. The grisliest deed came when Beggs threw the decapitated head into the sea while he was making his way over to Northern Ireland on the ferry. The butchery took place in Beggs' bedroom; when he had finished, it resembled an abattoir and had to be hastily redecorated by the Gay Ripper in order to conceal his acts of unimaginable horror.

The horrific bloodbath crime came about after homosexual Beggs had lured his victim back to his Kilmarnock flat. It wasn't until police divers on exercise in Loch Lomond discovered some body parts that the evil deed was discovered. Later, in December 1999, Barry's severed head washed up on an Ayrshire beach; a woman walking her dog made the ghastly discovery on Barassie Beach, near Troon.

Soon after, the cunning Beggs fled once more to his native Ireland before eventually making his way to Holland. Rather cleverly, he travelled via London, Jersey and France, hoping to send police on a false trail.

Beggs handed himself in to police in Amsterdam after Interpol launched a Europe-wide manhunt for him. When the case eventually came to trial, the jury was unaware that Beggs had already been jailed for killing a young, gay barman, called Barry Oldham. It occurred during 1987, when Beggs was studying public administration at Teesside Polytechnic – now Teesside University. He met Barry Oldham at a gay Newcastle nightclub. Police claim that he has also carried around twenty razor attacks on other gay men.

In a bizarre set of events, Beggs spent two years in prison before his conviction was quashed... on a technicality. At the 1987 trial, Beggs had insisted that the killing of Barry Oldham was carried out in self-defence.

However, Oldham's mutilated remains were found on the North Yorkshire Moors and Beggs was jailed for life for his murder.

The Crown applied to try him on a number of wounding charges involving other men alongside the murder charge. The judge at his trial, at Teesside Crown Court in December 1987, allowed the application – but the Court of Appeal said that he had been wrong to do so. At the appeal hearing in June 1989, the judges said: 'The prejudicial effect of these facts [on the charge of murder] must have been enormous.'

Two years later, Beggs slashed a young homosexual at his flat in Kilmarnock with a razor. He was caged for six years for this attack. The victim, Brian McQuillan, was so frightened of being killed that he jumped through a first-floor window to escape.

While awaiting sentencing, Beggs was sent to the secure state mental hospital at Carstairs, where he was given a detailed psychiatric examination.

All of this emerged after Beggs had been found guilty of the Limbs in the Loch murder; several of the jury shook their heads in wide-eyed disbelief. Surprisingly, when Beggs was shown graphic, photographic images of his victim's chopped up body, he openly wept in court.

Unsurprisingly, Beggs has been compared to the notorious Scots gay serial killer Dennis Nilsen. He is thought to have killed six others, including twenty-one-year-old student Colin Swiatek, who vanished after a night out with friends in 1997 at a gay Glasgow meeting place called Bennet's nightclub. The victim's body was found some months later in the River Clyde where Beggs was a regular visitor.

Detective Chief Superintendent Tony Fitzgerald, the North Yorkshire policeman who led the investigation into Barry Oldham's murder, has attributed further suspicious gay murders to Beggs.

During his time in Saughton Prison, Beggs, who has been labelled a predatory and cunning individual, found himself on the other end of a murder plot hatched by his fellow cons, who were incensed by the murder of Barry Wallace.

The plan to carve up Beggs was foiled when a makeshift knife was found during a spot search of the prison wing; the weapon would have been used to execute the bloodbath killer.

And that could well have been the end of that, except that, in March 2005, the cunning Beggs managed to get every government minister in Scotland declared in contempt of court! The unprecedented ruling was made at the Court of Session. The case stemmed from an incident in Peterhead Prison in 2003, when Beggs claimed that prison officers had breached his human rights by opening letters from his legal advisors. I am sure that we have not heard the last of this disgusting bastard Beggs.

ROY ARCHIBALD HALL

The mad killer butler, Roy Archibald Hall, was a native of Glasgow who was born in 1924. He worked his way up the proverbial ladder until he rubbed shoulders with the wealthy elite. So where did it all go horribly wrong for him? Well, for a man who could have become an archetypal, lovable rogue with a legendary status, serial murder was his downfall.

Fiction could not have come up with a better story: a bisexual conman, thief and murderer, Hall soon realised that he had an instinctive gift for crime – and quickly became a skilful jewel thief. His reputation grew following a succession of daring scams and he moved to London.

When he was there, he became a member of the glitzy London scene – a friend to lords and criminals alike as his risqué lifestyle attracted both attention and admiration. However, life took an unexpected turn when Roy met his first true love. He would never have known that such happiness could lead to a vicious and bloody murder. The killing tipped Roy over the edge; a series of brutal murders followed and Roy's days of freedom were soon numbered.

While Roy was free, he circulated on the city's celebrity gay scene, even claiming to have had affairs with Lord Boothby and the playwright Terence Rattigan. His first prison sentence came after he was found guilty of passing jewellery he had stolen in Perth. He would alternate between freedom and the clink – enjoying the champagne lifestyle when free and planning his next tryst while behind bars.

Eventually, Hall worked as butler to Lady Margaret Hudson at Kirtleton House, Dumfriesshire, and this is when he killed for the first time. The victim was a prison lover, David Wright, who joined Hall at the manor (a bad idea) and threatened to reveal his past (a worse idea).

Wright was shot dead on a rabbit hunt and was buried beneath boulders in a stream. One might excuse Hall for this slip from grace; he was not quite the psychopathic monster, yet.

Wright's removal was a licence to kill for Hall: he'd got away with murder. The seal was set and the worst was yet to come when he became butler to Walter Scott-Elliot, an elderly and wealthy former Labour MP and his wife Dorothy. These two went the same way as Wright – they were murdered.

While in the employ of Walter Scott-Elliot, Hall planned to drain the couple's bank accounts before going into retirement abroad. He blamed his partner Michael Kitto for the escalation of brutal violence. In what is thought to have been an unexpected situation, it was while Hall was showing Kitto around the swanky house of his boss that Scott-Elliot's wife confronted them.

Panic set in and Kitto, Hall later said, killed the woman by placing his hand over her mouth to stifle her screams. Soon, a whole catalogue of murders set in: it was a situation that had evolved from Hall having his eye set on a wealthy hit to suddenly becoming a character out of a Michael Winner *Death Wish* film.

In what would have been farcical if it were not true, Hall and Kitto set about feeding the old man sedatives and alcohol and then driving him up to Scotland, accompanied by Mary Coggles, a waitress and prostitute they knew. In the boot of the car was

Dorothy's body – they didn't bury it until they got near to Braco, in Perthshire.

They killed Scott-Elliot with a spade in a remote wood near Tomich, Invernesshire, shortly afterwards. I do not know whether murder induces sexual desire, but soon both Hall and Kitto were having sex with Mary Coggles. They then proceeded to kill her; she had become a liability in their eyes.

The killing spree was not quite finished. Hall's half-brother, Donald, was murdered when Hall used chloroform to subdue him, before drowning him in a bath at his holiday cottage in Newton Arlosh, Cumbria.

Hall's licence to kill was coming to an end. A worried hotel manager called the police when he thought Hall and Kitto were not going to pay their hotel bill. Hall made a mad dash out of a toilet window on the police's arrival, but was soon caught at a police roadblock. Hall received a minimum sentence of fifteen years and died in Kingston Prison in 2002, at the age of seventy-eight.

7

Bongo's Madness

What happens when a hard bastard really loses the plot...

BONGO McKLEISH

Bongo McKleish comes from one of the most deprived housing schemes in Glasgow. Easterhouse, one of the biggest housing projects in Europe, has been well documented over the years. Total violence is a way of life for the gang members there, to such an extent that one of the top American evangelists, Billy Graham, came to the housing scheme to call for peace among the locals.

Bongo comes from Drummy, the biggest part of the scheme. He was doing six months in Barlinnie Prison (the big house), when he and a few others were involved in the worst riot in the jail's history; another boy from Easterhouse, Shug Twigg also got wrapped up in the madness that seemed to possess the cons.

It didn't take long until all the screws had been rounded up and chased out of the hall at knifepoint. The plan hadn't been to take any hostages, but one screw was trapped between a rock and a hard place: he didn't manage to get out of the hall quickly enough, so he was taken hostage by the now-totally-out-of-control prisoners.

The cons held the warder hostage in one of the cells, hooded and bound, until they could break through one of the roofs of the cells on the top flat of the hall. That particular task didn't take them long; they worked together like a colony of ants. After they had cleared all of the rubble and roofing from the cell, the screw was marched, hooded and bound, up to the cell, where he received a few punches to the face from Bongo and Shug.

After the beating, the rioters decided to pull the screw up into the loft space of the hall; they knew that it would be much safer from there to keep the riot screws, who by now were milling around the bottom flat of the hall, at bay.

One of the prisoners came up with the bright idea of taking the cell doors off the cells. These doors were removed with reasonable ease: the hinges were only bolted onto old wooden frames and the prisoners stuck a few books between the hinges and then slammed the door shut as hard as they possible could. The hinges burst out of the frame. After removing some fifty doors, they knew the riot screws wouldn't dare to climb the stairs.

If the riot screws hadn't been wearing their protective hats and riot shields, there would definitely have been a number of deaths. After removing the doors that started on the little hallway on the flat, a couple of bangs later they managed to smash holes in the black lead slabs that were joined up to make a narrow pathway. The slabs fell onto the gantry of the third flats below.

Now the screws really had their work cut out. If they managed to dodge the doors and beds that were raining down on them from above, they still had the problem of walking the gantry: they would have to jump over the 15–20ft holes that the cons had made in them.

The cons knew that the riot screws weren't going to get to them in a hurry. To pass the time, Bongo and Shug decided to smash holes all over the roof of the hall, just for something to do. Bongo was the first con onto the roof, where, unknown to him, he was being filmed from a cell in the opposite hall. Not that he gave a fuck; he wasn't even wearing a mask to try and hide his identity. He was in his element, so was Shug, and to their credit, they didn't half wreck the roof of the hall. This riot and hostage siege went on for nearly four days... until the cons got pissed off and hungry.

Bongo was seen on the TV news all around Britain, standing on the roof with the screw's hat on and holding the hostage by the neck. The reason Bongo gave for giving himself up was probably the funniest conclusion to such a violent incident in history of any prison riot: he stood down after he spotted his girlfriend and child shouting up to him to end the siege.

Years later, I asked Bongo how his girlfriend had known that it was him from such a distance. His reply is legendary among us prisoners: he said that his girlfriend had recognised him by his swagger on the roof. In truth, Bongo really does have a rather distinctive walk.

When the siege ended, Bongo and Shug were placed in the Wendy House (solitary) and beaten. Any prisoner who has been in trouble in prison would have spent time in this seg unit. After the beatings, Bongo was given sleeping tablets in his dinner. When he was still out cold, the screws carried him into a van and took him some 250 miles north from Glasgow, to Peterhead seg block. When he woke up, he didn't know where he was. He had to lie there for the next eighteen months – in the winter, the snow and rain and wind blew through his cell window as there was no glass to keep the weather out. Bongo grew a beard and had to tie a poncho around his prison clothes to try and stay warm. There wasn't even a buzzer in his cell to alert the screws that he needed anything, there was just a piece of wood that was red at the tip. If he displayed it on the wall outside his cell, the screws knew that he wanted them. The screws didn't give a fuck, though. He didn't even see himself for eighteen months.

When he did finally see himself in a mirror, he didn't really know who he was; this sent him stir crazy for a little while but, through sheer determination, he pulled himself together. He went to Glasgow High Court with Shug and a couple of others and received the highest-possible sentence of ten years; he only had four weeks left of his six-month sentence when he got involved in the riot and hostage. He is well and out now and the last I heard he is doing OK.

Shug Twiggs, who got four years for his part in the riot, is also out, but, sadly, he is now off his head. The screws managed to break this boy's spirit. However, these two boys will always be heroes in Easterhouse.

8

Hard as Nails

`HAMMY´ HAMILTON

Martin 'Hammy' Hamilton is probably one of Scotland's best-known criminals. Everyone in Scotland has heard of him for a whole host of things. Most other prisoners and gangsters outside hate this man because he is a homosexual, but despite all the things that people say about him, no one can take it away from Hammy. He has carried out some of the best robberies anyone, perhaps with the exception of James Crosbie, has ever managed to achieve in Scotland.

I have known Hammy for years. He was once shot in the chest twice at point-blank range with a sawn-off shotgun. I would have loved to see the faces of the other hard men when Hammy then got out of the car and chased them with his own handgun. He has also been stabbed multiple times, both in and out of prison, but he is still standing. In fact, a young, up-and-coming boy called Billy stabbed Hammy four times in Glenochil Prison.

I asked Billy why he'd stabbed Hammy and he told me

that Hammy had been trying to touch him up and bully him. I don't know why Hammy would have wanted to do that, as young Billy's hardly an oil painting. Whatever happened, Billy was charged with attempted murder for the attack.

I was in Glenochil in 1992 when Hammy was stabbed five times in the chest and belly by a man called Fudge but, give Hammy his dues, he didn't try to turn his attacker in. Fudge was never punished for his frenzied attack on Hammy. And things got no better for him: he also had pit bulls and Rottweilers set on him and, guess what? He beat the dogs. He's a hard bastard, Hammy.

He is, by far, one of the unluckiest criminals in Scottish criminal history. He received a life sentence in November 2000, not because he had committed a murder, but because the Scottish Crown and MSPs wanted him off the streets – he was considered far too dangerous to be left walking about free.

I have known Hammy for years and, as I have said, I haven't personally got anything against him. Rumour has it that he has murdered at least eight or ten men, but they are only rumours. He has also walked out free from seven High Court trials for bank robberies; he must have been doing something right.

Hammy has lodged an appeal against his life sentence and I really hope he wins it. It doesn't matter if you like this legendary criminal or not, he doesn't deserve to be doing a life sentence if he has never been charged with killing anyone.

Hammy is no stranger to dishing out some real nasty

violence in prison, though. He spent a stint of four years in the seg units because the other prisoners were paranoid about having him in among them. There have been so many stories of him assaulting people at knifepoint.

All I can say is that whenever I have ever been in with him, any boys that have been up to his cell have done so under their own steam. Sticking knives at innocent boys' necks and assaulting them? It's total piss, an urban myth. I am not sticking up for Hammy, I'm just not going to slag him off.

STEWART BOYD

Another man of sheer violence was the late Stewart Boyd. He was killed in a car accident over in Spain's Costa del Sol shortly after his release from prison in June 2003. While he was alive, he certainly left his mark on the city streets of Glasgow. He was a force to be reckoned with, a real gang enforcer. Murder and witness intimidation were high on his criminal charge sheet. In 1997, he was cleared of murdering the Paisley gangster Mark Rennie, but was jailed in 2001 for threatening security firm boss John Jeffrey during the trial of his associate, Lewis Rodden, who was later shot dead in an Amsterdam strip joint.

GARY MOORE

Gary Moore is another legendary figure of sheer violence that spent most of his adult life inside one jail or another.

When, on the odd occasion, he does get out of prison, it isn't too long before he embarks on a murderous campaign of total terror. Gary has been charged and stood trial for some three or four different murders. For instance, when he was charged for the murder, along with his friend Dagor Clark, of a prostitute called Diane McCanally, the case was dropped through a lack of evidence.

The coppers in Glasgow hate Gary so much that he is their prime suspect for every murder that takes place. The truth is that, more times than not, Gary isn't even in the city at the time these murders take place.

Gary's violence is legendary in the prison system; he can go to any jail in Scotland and demand the highest respect from the top men there. He is also a very smart man. When he was in Perth Prison doing eight years, he was told that Jimmy Boyle's boy, James, was going with his girlfriend. Gary kept his head down and walked about with a Bible under his arm for nine months, going to church and prayer meetings.

He had pulled the wool over the Perth screws' eyes because, on his first four-hour home leave, Gary went round to his girlfriend's flat in the south side of Glasgow to pay a visit on his little girl. He was dotty about her, but when Gary was in prison, James Boyle – Jimmy Boyle's son – wouldn't let Gary's kid visit him. It was the only excuse that Gary needed.

Gary knocked on the door and when Boyle Jr opened it, Gary stabbed him clean through the heart and neck. Boyle made a dash after him down the stairs, but collapsed and died at the bottom of them.

Gary picked Boyle up and flung the body, head first, into a big steel wheelie bin. He then made his way back up to the flat to visit his little girl. Gary was soon caught and taken to Barlinnie's seg unit, where he remained until his murder trial. Now, you would think that it would have been a guaranteed life sentence. Well, it just goes to show you how clever Gary was: in 1994, he was sentenced to just seven years for killing the son of probably the most well-known Scottish gangster.

The papers were very nasty towards Gary, calling him names such as 'Ogre' Moore. He is, in fact, the total opposite of that. He has now finished his sentence and is currently walking the streets of Glasgow as a free man.

BRIAN BEUFFORD TAGGART

I met Brian Beufford Taggart in Glenochil Prison back in 1992. He was well spoken and immaculately groomed for a prisoner. I didn't know Beufford from Adam, but after a couple of nights spent talking with him at the seg unit doors, I soon got the gist of who this man was.

Beuff lived in Easterhouse, one of the roughest, hardest parts of Glasgow, where he had built up a name for himself as a 'have-a-go', meaning he didn't take any shit. That was certainly true. I was with Beuff constantly over the next few years and there is no doubt that he had the respect of all the other prisoners and screws.

Until Hammy Hamilton arrived on the scene, after he got nine years for robbing yet another bank, Beuff ran the hall. They were at loggerheads before too long and you didn't need to be a rocket scientist to see that something nasty was going to happen between them.

I stuck with my big friend through thick and thin and when the war between Beuff and Hammy finally kicked off, I was only twenty-three years old. At first it was just tit-for-tat strikes at their rival's henchmen.

I can clearly remember one particular time when Beuff and his other friend, Frazer McDowell, went to the gym to do their weights workout, just as they would have done any other day of the week.

Unbeknown to them, Hammy had told a couple of his top henchmen, one of whom was a guy called Hendy, to set about Beuff and Frazer. They walked into the weights room and started to play a mind game with Beuff and Frazer. Hendy was no mug himself and he toyed with the two and made them feel uneasy. I would just like to state, I am friendly with Hendy and I'm not going to have a dig at him like others might do. The only people I have a dig at are the ones who I still have issues with.

Anyway, Hendy set up some 80kg on his bar, then lay down to bench-press the quite heavy weight. Beuff and Frazer took their chance to attack Hendy – instead of the other way round – and, by fuck, they didn't half attack him. Hendy had the bar on his chest when Beuff and Frazer ran the 10ft or so with 20kg weight bars in their hands, before they simultaneously smashed them into Hendy's face and head.

Now remember, Hendy already had 80kg of steel on his chest when he was struck by the bars; they opened the boy's head and face up like a burst tomato but, to give

Hendy his dues, he still managed to get up off the bench and struggle out of the weights' room before falling out cold on the ground outside.

Hendy was rushed to hospital and spent some five weeks in intensive care before he returned to prison wearing what resembled a scaffold, which was there to hold the broken bones in his face together. It should be stated that Hendy didn't say a word to the coppers who were now treating the assault as an attempted murder. Beuff and Frazer got away with the incident in the gym hall scot-free.

A high percentage of fights and slashings are played out in the PT halls. I can say, thankfully, that Hendy made a total recovery. I am glad of that: the man didn't deserve to have been smashed over the head and face so brutally, but that's what happens in prisons. It's a dog-eat-dog world.

Beuff and Frazer returned to the hall and turned their attention to Hammy himself. Somehow they managed to get a tin of CS gas smuggled into the prison, but Hammy had a little surprise of his own up his sleeve. He managed to get hold of a bottle of sulphuric acid. It was going to be all-out war between the two camps.

At this point the story takes a bizarre twist. One of Hammy's closest pals at the time, Mo Morrison, was secretly going behind his back and working with Beuff and Frazer, because they were supplying him with more smack than his friend Hammy.

If Hammy had known what Mo was doing at the time, he would certainly have tried to take him out of the game, but Hammy was oblivious; he gave Mo the acid and told

him to run in and fling it over the two 'proclaimers' –
Hammy and his camp's nickname for Beuff and Frazer.
But Beuff and Frazer also had plans for Mo; they had
earmarked him for running into his own camp's cell to
spray them with the CS gas.

After that had been done, the plan was for all of us to
run into the cell and stab Hammy's camp to death... and
I mean death. That is exactly what Hammy had in mind
for our camp as well. It was due to take place at 6.30pm,
once the screws had come back from their tea breaks.
However, someone – I don't know who – must have taken
a parra attack and told one of the screws what was going
to happen.

As 6.30pm arrived, the screws kept the cell doors
shut. Rather than letting us out, they did cell searches
instead and discovered both the CS gas and the acid.
Hammy was removed to the seg unit; Beuff and Frazer
were kept in their cells until being moved to different seg
units in Scotland.

When I look back at it all now, I have to say that I'm
rather glad it never really kicked off into an all-out
bloodbath; some of us would no doubt be sitting here on
lifers for murdering other prisoners and I have no doubt
that a few cons would have lost their lives that night.

Beuff is out of prison now and is running a very
successful business. Frazer is just finishing off a seven-
year sentence, after being involved in a high-speed car
crash, which cost three people their lives. Hendy is
finishing off six years: he was stabbed in the chest when
he took a ten-minute nap in the laundry shed in Perth

Prison where he was always having run-ins with some unsavoury character or another.

I haven't seen or heard from Beuff for some years now, but I still write to his little brother Taggs, who is doing eleven years in prison after being caught in possession of £175-worth of heroin. Young Taggs is a bit of a boy himself.

Mo is the legendary Duster Morrison's boy, who I have already told you about. He was one of the first boys to be told he was HIV positive in Glenochil and is currently finishing off yet another twelve-year sentence for his part in a robbery. I like Mo, as we have been through far too much together, but a lot of cons don't like him because he is a bandit who, over the years, has been responsible for robbing more boys in prison with his gang than the legendary Robin Hood himself. It isn't just daft little boys he has robbed either; some of his victims are very, very hard men. I wish them all well, whatever they are doing now and hope that they can stay out of prison this time. Respect, Jimmy Boy.

MICK REZELLI

Mick Rezelli stands only 5ft 4in tall, but whatever this man lacks in height, he certainly makes up for in courage. Everyone knows Mick, both in and out of prison, because he is infamous for two things.

Mick was being remanded in Barlinnie's C-Hall for bank robbery when he decided that enough was enough. He wanted to go home to Drumchaple – a carbon copy of Easterhouse and Castlemick, that is, a very rough place to live – so he started to put his plans in motion. He began sawing his cell bars, day in, day out, and after two weeks of constant sawing, he was finally ready. However, he had another problem: he didn't have enough bed sheets to make his rope long enough – the sheets he had left him with a 20ft drop to the ground, outside the hall.

Give this man credit, he went ahead, took his chances and became the first person in the jail's history to escape from a locked cell – you will read about the others later, but their mode of escape was different to Mick's.

When he landed, he twisted his ankle, but that didn't put him off. He managed to climb up onto the wall at the old stairwell that led to the lawyers' offices. After he was on the wall of the prison, he dropped down to the ground – a fall of 40ft. When he landed, he broke his ankle completely. Most others would have thrown the towel in because of the sheer pain, but not this legendary robber: he hobbled and hopped away into a garden, where he lay for the next twenty-nine hours, with no water and with his ankle snapped in two places. His determination pulled him through the ordeal.

When the coast was clear, he flagged down a passing taxi and went to Drumchaple. When Mick left the taxi, he disappeared into a maze of safe houses. A couple of his close friends put a homemade plaster cast on his foot. No one would have expected the ankle to heal properly, but it did.

The second thing about little Mick that places him a cut above most other hard men is his self-belief. When he was just a young man, around twenty or so, he was shot in the face with a double-barrelled sawn-off shotgun. The pellets entered his forehead and cheek – where some are still lodged to this day – but you could never tell by looking at him. After the gunman had fired the gun and run out of the pub, Mick ran out after him and shot the man, before he had to sit on the ground as he was losing too much blood. Thankfully, he made a complete recovery from the shotgun wounds on his face. The last I heard, the little chap was doing well outside, and long may it continue. A true hard-wearing bastard.

JED MALLOY

Wee Jed Malloy is currently out of prison. He stands only 5ft tall, but is another man with the heart of a Scottish lion, despite the fact that he is actually Irish.

He is the most dangerous leprechaun I have ever met. When I first met Jed, once again in Glenochil Prison, I couldn't help but notice his scar wounds – about ninety per cent of his face is covered in scars. This happened when two brothers from his area in Parkhead, called the Watsons – who themselves are nobody's fools – cornered Jed in the toilet of their local pub.

Jed pulled his lock-back knife out to toe-to-toe it with them, but these men stood 5ft 7in tall and they managed to get Jed on the floor of the toilet. When they had got him there, he was held down by his arms by one and the other sat astride him, slashing his face repeatedly until there was no visible skin tissue left. Jed lapsed into unconsciousness through blood loss.

Once he got to hospital, he went underwent emergency surgery, where the doctors put in some 500 stitches to hold his skin on. When this little man left hospital, he wasn't going to accept what the brothers had done, so he went looking for them.

When he found one of the brothers, he ran up to him brandishing a gun and pulled the trigger, but luckily for the boy, Jed's gun jammed. Later that night, though, the gun didn't jam and Jed shot a bouncer in the mouth and throat, critically injuring him. Jed was now on a rampage: he had shot the bouncer because he had hit his little cousin and because he had been calling Jed all sorts of derogatory names.

As if this wasn't enough, the little chap started a running battle with another gang. This run-in continued until Jed and his family murdered one of their rivals. I met Jed's young cousins, Steph McEndrie and Alan Brown, in prison as well and they are just as dangerous as Jed. I am still very, very pally with Steph and I class this man as my true brother.

Anyway, Jed got jumped in prison by a monster-sized prisoner called Pinny – this man stood 6ft 7in tall – yet Pinny still had to go in with two knives taped to his hands. He stabbed Jed six times; one of the wounds was just two inches from the little man's heart but, thankfully, he made a total recovery.

Anyone who is anyone knows Jed and his family. They are legends in the Parkhead area of Glasgow's rough East End. Alan Brown, Jed's cousin, has now settled down with his wife and two kids. And Steph, as I have said, is like my brother. Along with his girl Sharon, he used to visit me when I was behind bars and he always made sure that I didn't want for anything. Not many people stand by their friends the way that Steph and Sharon have stood by me and I can only say thanks. Both Steph and I know that we would take a bullet for each other and I would certainly visit him every week if he was in prison. Big it up, brother. Sharon, I love you with all my heart as well. You have been my rock. God bless you all.

9

Years, Years, Years

`TOSSO´ KINNING

Tony 'Tosso' Kinning started off doing twelve years. As a result of numerous indiscretions he ended up getting another twelve years. What is so significant about this man is that he did eleven solid years in one solitary confinement unit or another up and down Scotland – and that must be a Scottish prison record.

I know that Tam McCulloch has spent twenty-nine years in solitary, but he had everything he wanted there and was also allowed to walk about his unit when he wanted and could cook his own food. It wasn't the same for Tosso and those years really took their toll on him: he couldn't really communicate with others and his eyes wandered all over the place when you talked to him but, apart from that, he has somehow managed to retain all his marbles.

I have seen boys end up in the nut house after three to six months of solitary, so just think how strong-minded Tosso must have been to have spent all that time in the concrete tomb. He rolled about with the riot screws every day for the first two years.

Tosso loves his yoga, and this must have helped him through the long, hard, and very cold winters up in the Peterhead cellblock. The screws couldn't get him in their arm locks too easily either, due to his yoga fitness and flexibility. He was released after his twenty-four-year sentence but, sadly, he is now back inside doing fifteen years for robbery. I hope you can manage to do this sentence in mainstream without any clowns trying to rub you up the wrong way and, for your sake, I hope that the screws don't try their daft mind games with you. However, I know you'll end up doing something that you don't want to do. Anyway, keep your chin up and sail through this one in the same way that all the other people you know are doing. Respect.

BLAVA

Blava comes from Govan in the southside of Glasgow and is still serving his life sentence. I got really close to this diamond man and I can tell you that he is no man's mug. Inside the walls of the Scottish prison system, he is a force to be reckoned with but Blava doesn't jump about the prison like a hard man, unlike so many others I could mention in this book.

You see, there are a lot of myths about certain people and the things that they are supposed to have done, when, in actual fact, they haven't lifted their hands to anyone. This isn't the case with Blava: he's a con's con, through and through.

ROBERT O'HARA

Robert O'Hara, who is better known as the 'Birdman', is twenty-seven years old and comes from Possil Park in the north of Glasgow. Birdman recently got sentenced to twenty years in prison for his part in a murder that he had nothing to do with. You see, because he had always been one step ahead of the cops, they had never been able to pin anything on him. This pissed them off big time so, when one of Birdman's crew stabbed a rival gang member to death, the shit really hit the fan – for both the Birdman and his crew.

It was reported in the national press that a stash of guns had been recovered from a house in Cumbernauld – it included one Mac10 snubnose gun, two revolvers and a 9mm. The drugs squad also recovered over £150,000 that had been hidden under the floorboards. Not surprisingly, the gang had to go on the run.

Birdman and his good lady went to Mexico for a holiday to lie low for a while, but as soon as they stepped back on Scottish soil, the bold Birdman was arrested and charged with the brutal murder. The rest of his gang were also soon rounded up.

In total, the Birdman and his crew received sentences ranging from twenty years to ten years. And this is where Scottish law is so corrupt: the Birdman, who hadn't even committed the murder, was the one who received the twenty-year sentence.

Throughout the course of his young life, the Birdman has been shot three times and survived. Without a shadow of a doubt, had it not been for his incarceration, he would have gone on to rule the north end of Glasgow, Maryhill and Springburn, along with his close friend Paul McGovern, the current head of the infamous family clan, who, at just sixteen years of age, was sentenced to life for the knife murder of an older man in Springburn.

But back to the Birdman: it wasn't too long before the gang member who had actually murdered the rival was stabbed in prison – allegedly on the Birdman's orders – to within an inch of his life. Quite right, too: he had cost the Birdman twenty years of his life when he hadn't even been there when the murder took place. I would just like to say a couple of words to Birdman. I hope you win your appeal, mate, as you are an innocent man and everyone here knows it. I wish you all the luck in the world to beat this corrupt Scottish system. Yours, Jimmy Boy. Big up, mate.

GOGS SMITH

I only met Gogs Smith a few years ago, when I was in Shotts, and he looked nothing like I had imagined him to look. Gogs spent a total of nine years in solitary with his friend Tosso, before they ended up falling out big time. Gogs was serving nineteen years for his part in a robbery and he was famous for his quick temper. He has calmed down considerably over the last few years and is finishing off a four-year sentence – he received that after having done a nineteen-year stretch. He gains my complete and utter respect for the nine years he spent in total solitary.

JIM WILKINSON

Jim Wilkinson comes from a small village in Ayrshire called Prestwick. He has recently been released from his life sentence, but while he was in prison, he got a total of nineteen years added to his life sentence for his part in two major riots in Peterhead and Perth prisons. Everyone in the system knew and respected this man. He may only stand 5ft 5in tall, but what he lacks in height he more than makes up for in heart. He is a very violent man, indeed, so much so, that he was kept in segregation for over five years.

HARRY MITCHELL

Harry Mitchell, who comes from Dundee, is some character. Over the last twenty-five years, Harry has only been out of prison for three of them. While he was in prison, the big man got into a heated argument with some heavy men from Glasgow, and Harry, being the man he is, was up for going all the way with them, if need be.

If he had had any sort of inkling as to what lay ahead, I'm not sure that he would have gone to the PT hall that day: there waiting for him was the man from Glasgow and his three friends. Harry flung one of his massive hands into the rival's chin and KO'd the smaller man, but that is when things started to go pear-shaped.

The three other men pulled out three 8in jail daggers made of solid steel that had been sharpened into points at one end.

Harry had no place to go, so he tried his best to protect

himself from the frenzied attack that rained down on him; he didn't stand a snowball's chance in hell of walking or running out of the PT hall in one piece. He received thirty-seven wounds to his head, neck and torso and when his assailants had finished their attack, they left him for dead, covered his body with aerobics mats and walked coolly out into the shower rooms. The head PT instructor found Harry after his head count of prisoners came up one short.

Thanks to his quick thinking and first-aid skills, as well as the prison nurse's dedication, Harry survived the brutal knife attack. On his way to the hospital, Harry died twice, but the paramedics managed to bring him back to life. In hospital, he received twenty-seven pints of blood. Thankfully, though, he went on to make a full recovery.

Harry is probably one of the most violent men in and around Dundee. He is rumoured to have taken a 4x4 jeep from a well known drug dealer over a drugs debt. When the big man received ten years for robbing a chemist with his co-accused, things went wrong, but Harry got the man back for grassing him up to the cops.

As soon as Harry got out of prison, he took his co-accused hostage and beat him with a meat cleaver. Now, if that wasn't bad enough, the big man then tied the grass's hands together and flung him into the River Tay.

The only thing that saved the co-accused's life was the current; it swept the unconscious man's body onto the embankment, where he was spotted by a man walking his dog. He quickly alerted the cops, who in turn called out the paramedics.

You can see why Harry has got such a name for being dangerous and unpredictable both in and around Dundee.

STEVIE NISBET

Stevie Nisbet, currently eighteen years into his life sentence, is a well-known hood. His cousin, JH, was shot dead, along with his friend, when they went to meet a couple of other men over a drugs deal. JH had just committed a robbery on a security van and had taken in the region of £800,000, so he now found himself in the super league of the crime world.

However, people in the Wishaw area in Lanarkshire then tried to take them out. On one occasion, a knife-wielding team poured out of a car and tried to stab them. Luckily, they survived that hit but, two months later, JH wasn't so lucky.

Stevie took revenge on someone who was supposed to have been involved in his cousin's murder. However, by the time he found out that the man hadn't had anything to do with it, it was too late. Along with his friends Quinny and Dom, Stevie received an eighteen-year sentence.

ALAN DOWELL

Alan Dowell is probably Edinburgh's most well-known hard man. He has done two ten-year sentences, back to back, for numerous acts of violence and robbery and is a giant of a man with umpteen bare-knuckle fights under his belt.

Any team in Scotland or south of the border would be well pleased to have such a violent gangster as Alan on their books. In Edinburgh, his name alone opens doors in nightspots all over the city.

I believe he has settled down with his new wife, who he met while he was behind bars in the Shotts special unit. Good luck to him as well, as he is not getting any younger. Don't get me wrong: he is not short of a few bob, thanks to the many friends he made during his years in prison. Good luck for the future, mate.

RONNIE ALDRED

Ronnie Aldred is yet another well-known man from the Scottish capital and has done more time than the three bears. To be fair, Ronnie *is* the size of a bear and has a heart to go with it. He has just received yet another twelve-year sentence for taking two men hostage over a drugs deal that went wrong. Ronnie tortured the men over a two-day period, during which he pulled one of the men's teeth out with a pair of pliers.

When Ronnie was on remand in Saughton Prison, he was repeatedly stabbed while talking to his wife on the phone. He was oblivious to the fact that he had been stabbed, thinking that it had only been one of his pals fooling around and it was only when he came off the phone and toppled over that he realised what had happened. No wonder. This man is 19st, although it is not all muscle. All the same, Ronnie went to wreak revenge on his attacker. However, the coward had run into his cell and slammed the door shut. Ronnie couldn't get his revenge. The screws soon got wind of the stabbing, but Ronnie played it down, even though he had four puncture wounds in his neck and back. He is a close friend of Alan Dowell.

JOCK DONALDSON

Jock Donaldson, who has done eighteen years of his life sentence, is a legendary figure in the Scottish prison system. I have met him once, in Shotts, and we have a mutual friend, Old Hugh Boyd. Hugh's youngest son, Sid, God bless him, was my close pal before he died of an overdose.

When Jock was in Shotts special unit back in the early nineties, just after the place had opened, he got into a heated argument with a couple of the screws. One thing led to another before Jock totally lost the plot and stabbed one of the screws to the hilt with a knife and slashed another one. To look at him, you wouldn't think that Jock was a violent man but, please believe me, this man is ultra-violent. It just goes to show how you should never judge a book by its cover.

I was in the Peterhead seg unit with Jock in 1998, but I didn't know him then. However, I knew about most of the things he had done in prison and I have got nothing but total, 100 per cent respect for him. At one stage, he did some six-and-a-half years in solitary confinement. Any man who does that kind of lock-up gets my utmost respect, as long as he isn't a monster, that is.

I can now, gladly, say that Jock is down in Kilmarnock

and doing really well. If he can keep his head down, hopefully he will be out of the door before his twentieth year in prison is finished. Jock, I wish you all the best, my friend.

ADGER

Adger has now served twenty-eight years of his life sentence. For some reason, though, this man isn't too well liked among the other prisoners. He isn't a sex case or a monster, so I don't know why people don't really like him, but there is one thing that no one can take away from him: he has done years at a time in the seg units. In total, he must have spent fourteen or sixteen years in them – although not all in one go. As I write, he is still in the Shotts seg unit.

Adger has legendary strength: he has ripped doors off their hinges, windows out and bed frames away from the bolts that hold them to the ground, single-handedly. This guy spends all day, every day, doing press-ups, sit-ups and yoga. He was convicted for the murder of a dwarf. Once he had killed him, he cut off the dwarf's arms and legs and stuffed them into the back of a 24in colour TV. I am not kidding about this. It may sound bizarre, but it's 100 per cent the truth.

ANDY WALKER

Andy 'The Soldier' Walker was in Shotts seg unit back in 1999. When I met him, he had already served three years of a sentence that had been reduced from thirty years to twenty-seven when he was placed in the Shotts special unit. The former Royal Scots corporal had been convicted of fatally shooting three of his Army pals. While he was still on the Army's payroll, he, along with three others, had been ordered to transfer some money to the bank. Andy had other ideas, however, and shot his colleagues. He then tried to make it look as though some sort of robbery had taken place, but he was always the main suspect in the police's eyes.

Andy has a bad heart. He had a heart attack in the Shotts seg and another in the Shotts special unit. He also had a mild one a few winters ago when we were involved in a running battle with the screws. Andy was the longest-serving prisoner in the history of the Shotts special unit. All in, he has spent eleven and a half years there and during that time has formed some close friendships with the screws.

Danny Boyle, Billy Lewis, and I got on OK with Andy, the old one, anyway. But something changed. I don't know what got into him, as he used to get involved in rooftop riots and knife fights with other prisoners... not any more. Maybe he just wants to live a quiet life and serve out his very long sentence. You can't take it away from him, though, he serves his time with a spring in his step and if he started being friendlier with other prisoners then he would be spot on. Even though Andy talks to screws more often than most prisoners, I still give him respect for the way he has done his time.

THE LOCKERBIE BOMBER

Abdelbaset Ali Mohmed al-Megrahi is Scotland's worst-ever multiple killer but, let's be truthful, no prisoner really believes that this man carried out the Lockerbie bombing, despite the fact that he must have had played a bit-part somewhere in the carry-on. He is doing twenty-seven years rec for killing 270 innocent British and American people and is currently in Barlinnie Prison, in his own state-of-the-art, purpose-built special unit. Who knows, by the time this book has gone to print he may well already have won his appeal; there's some pretty dodgy stuff about the whole incident that hasn't been fully revealed. Even if he loses the appeal, he may well be sent back to his own country to serve his time.

He isn't allowed to see any other prisoners, but if anyone back in Libya had done what he was supposed to have done, then they would have had a bullet in the back of the head by now.

I was in Barlinnie's seg unit when Nelson Mandela came to visit this man and he was reported to have said that al-Megrahi is being held in inhuman conditions. Well Nelson, no disrespect, but wake up and smell the coffee: you should have taken a look in the seg unit that we all have to spend our time in for years on end. I used to respect you when you were in prison and I sang the 'Free Nelson Mandela' song along with everybody else, but now I don't even want to think of you – you are clearly just like the rest of them.

This bomber has got two Sky dishes, a TV, video, cooker, fridge, computer and his own fresh fruit and veg every day; all that for killing 270 people. I have never killed anyone and I am not alone: there are thousands of us who are all being treated like caged animals and eating filth that amounts more to slops than it does to food.

If I had killed ten people, I would want what this multiple murderer has when I came back inside. Do you really believe for one minute that anyone would get treated like him? No way. Just take a look at the innocent people who have been locked up like animals in Guantanamo Bay by the Americans. These people aren't even allowed a phone call, but this bastard who was found guilty – even though I have doubts as to whether he actually planted the bomb – is being treated like royalty when there are deserving people living rough on the streets of our cities.

What is going on with the law and justice? Andy Walker killed three men and is sentenced to thirty years in prison. This Libyan is convicted of killing 270 people and does twenty-seven years in a hotel leisure complex. It makes me boil with rage.

RICARDO BLANCO

Spaniard Ricardo Blanco and his two co-accused were the first people in Scotland to have been found guilty of murder without a body ever being found. Ricardo is no stranger to the Scottish prison system and has got into trouble with the screws and prisoners on numerous occasions.

On one occasion, he did a sneaky on Sammy 'The Bear' Ralston in Glenochil's PT hall. This man ran in and stabbed Sammo while he was having a shower, but to Sammo's credit, he didn't fall; instead, he turned and chased Ricardo out of the shower room. Sammo lifted a weight bar and started hitting the Spaniard over the head and back. The PT instructors broke it up.

When Ricardo went to Greenock, he went out on home leave with a screw to see his new wife and then went on the run for some four or five days before handing himself in. Most other prisoners hate Ricardo for some reason. He has now served sixteen years of his lifer, but there is a rumour that he is wanted in Spain for two other murders. I don't know whether this is true or not, but one thing is certain: this man will always be in some sort of trouble.

10

Great
Escapers

JOE STEELE

I am going to start this chapter with Joe Steele, as he has been involved in probably the most high profile escapes in Scottish prison history. When Joe escaped from Saughton Prison, he then went on the run down to England.

Joe didn't escape to stay on the run, like most other prisoners; he did it to highlight his case of injustice. By the time he embarked on this particular run, he had already served some thirteen years in prison.

After his friends had held a protest through the streets of London, Joe took it one step further. He alerted the press and TV crews that he would be turning himself in at a famous location in London. No one could have expected Joe to superglue his hands to the gates – not }just any old gates, but the world-famous gates of Buckingham Palace!

When the security teams came to move him on, they couldn't, as his hand had set fast in the super-strong glue. I watched the whole event on the TV news, along with everybody else in Scotland and Britain. Joe had certainly brought his case to clear his and TC Campbell's name, for the six murders they had wrongly been convicted for, to the public eye.

Joe stood proudly with his by-now-famous 'Free the Glasgow 2' t-shirt on. After he gave himself up, it wasn't too long before he got away again. This time, Joe climbed up the radio mast outside the front gates of Scotland's biggest prison and stood at the top of the mast shouting his innocence. He remained there for some four or five hours before agreeing to come back down. When he did come down, Joe made sure the TV news cameramen got all the shots they wanted of him. What this remarkable man did to highlight his and TC's innocence is legendary in the Scottish prison system.

Some years earlier, Joe's brothers made a great escape from Barlinnie, sliding down a rope, one end of which had been tied onto the chimney of one of the halls and the other tied onto the towbar of a car. When the car reversed, the rope tightened to allow them all to slide, one after the other, to their freedom. Fuck, all their escapes should be made into a movie! Never mind David Blaine and Houdini, remember the Steeles.

DANNY

Another man, Danny, had just been sentenced to sixteen years for his part in robbing three banks and a security van. When he was in Barlinnie Prison, Danny had a pipe dream about getting himself free. And that is exactly what

he did. Over a three-week period, he got his wife to bring
him in a long, brown wig, a skirt, a blouse, a set of false
boobs and a jacket.

The visit room back in those days was in the old PT hall
across from B-Hall. Danny's wife stashed the stuff in the
toilets; the screws didn't even look in the place. That night
Danny decided to make his escape bid. He went over to
the visit hall when the place was full, walked into the
toilet and quickly got out of his prison uniform and into
his female disguise.

The plan was for one of the prisoners to start an
argument with another prisoner and then for them to
start fighting, in the hope that this would cause a
distraction for long enough for Danny to get out, in
among the other visitors that would be escorted from the
jail during the mayhem. What a buzz that must have
been: here he was dressed up as a bird walking straight
out the front gates of Scotland's biggest prison. This took
place only as recently as 1987 or 1988.

Once the screws knew that Danny was missing, they
closed the prison down. However, it was already too late.
After having been sentenced to all those years in jail,
Danny was out again within two months. What a kick in
the balls that must have been for the screws, governors,
courts and MPs.

He then sent a postcard to the *News of the World*
saying: 'Wish you were here.' The postcard showed a
picture of the Costa del Sol, although, in actual fact
Danny had never left Glasgow. Danny was captured after
a few months and sent back to Barlinnie Prison: he got a

hero's welcome from the cons – and even from some of the screws – on his return.

Danny still holds the record for robbing three banks, one after the other, on the same day. Which reminds me, Willie Sutton was a notorious bank robber of the 1930s who, when asked why he robbed banks, answered simply: 'Because that's where the money is.'

Back to Danny, though: he is well out of the door now and has settled down with his wife and kids. Best of luck, pal, and I give you all the respect in the world. You are a legend among legends.

MICK HEALY

Mick Healy is still in prison down south. He started off with a ten-year sentence for his part in a robbery. Mick is one of Scotland's most prolific hard men robbers and is from the old school. What is so unique about this man is that he is the only person in the history of Shotts Prison to have ever got away from the prison successfully.

Mick was working in the prison cookhouse when he noticed that the same meat lorry came to the prison every week. You know the type: one of those four-ton lorries with a portable fridge freezer to keep the meat at the right temperature. When the driver opened the back door to bring the meat out, Mick and some of the other prisoners helped unload the stuff.

When there were only two or three little trays of meat remaining in the lorry, Mick made his move. He knew that it was going to be both a very cold and extremely uncomfortable ride, but it was worth it. Mick positioned himself under big joints of meat to hide himself from the screws when they checked in the back of the lorry before its departure.

Mick didn't dare to try and move from his hideout. After the lorry had left the prison, he just sat there, frozen, for the twenty-five- or thirty-minute journey back to Glasgow.

When the driver opened the back door, he got the fright of his life when he saw Mick jump out like a greyhound coming out of the traps. Mick knew immediately that he was in Duke Street; what's more, until the lorry driver rang them to let them know that a prisoner had just jumped out of the back of the lorry, the prison hadn't even noticed Mick's absence.

The coppers quickly arrived on the scene, but it was too late; Mick was long gone. To evade capture, Mick dressed up as a woman – the rumour goes that he made a lovely looking one as well.

Mick managed to stay on the run for a couple of years until, along with some other very well-known Glasgow hard men robbers, he was caught red-handed in a bank in Torquay. Mick ended up getting sentenced to some twenty-seven years; the gang that did the robbery with him all got sentences upwards of fourteen years. Mick's brother got a jail term as well, but I'm glad to say that Mick should be back on the streets sometime in 2006. I hope so. He is a true legend in Scottish crime history and I'm sure that quite a lot of English hard men have also heard about Mick and his legendary gang of robbers.

JIM WILLIAMSON

Jim Williamson is better known as 'Forty-niner' and has now served some eighteen or nineteen years of his life sentence. He started his prison life up in Peterhead back in the eighties and it wasn't too long before he had made a bit of a name for himself by always being the first person in to have a fight with any of the old Peterhead screws who thought they were harder than all the cons.

Jim comes from Ayrshire, and he was no mug. He took part in a riot, seized a hostage and ended up getting eight years on top of his life sentence. After this, he was moved to Glenochil Prison and this is where I met him. Jim, like so many of the other prisoners who have a name for violence, doesn't fit the stereotypical mould. He's a rather short, stumpy-looking man with one of the widest smiles I have ever seen. He also had some good friends on the outside that always made sure that he was provided with drugs.

After a few years, this man had changed into a drug-fuelled monster who would do anything to get his hands on smack, just like the rest of us, me included. However, I would never have thought that Jim could have ended up so mad with drugs.

Jim was involved in the fall-out after my little friend Rab Leslie had his eye taken out by Pat Flynn with a knife. Rab wasn't happy and drew up a battle plan to get his revenge on Pat and his whole camp of friends. I was supposed to take one of them out myself, but I will not say who, I'll just leave them guessing. Another one of my friends, Budgie from Port Glasgow who was camped

216

up with Rab, Sid and I, was designated as the one to take Jim out.

Although Jim had never done anything to Sid, Budgie or I, he had become a legitimate target because his friend had taken Rab's eye out. It just so happens that little Budgie was working in the boat shed along with Jim Forty-niner. Jim was pally with little Budgie and was blissfully unaware of what was about to happen. Jim always used to call Budgie into the toilet for a burn of kit on the foil and on the day that it all kicked off, it was no different. Jim shouted Budgie in on the dot, like clockwork.

Budgie slipped his 10in jail dagger from his waistband to his sleeve for quicker access and when he sat down next to Jim, he didn't waste any time. He pulled the dagger from his sleeve and drove it deep into Jim's side, straight up to the hilt, the full ten inches.

Jim couldn't move. Budgie removed the knife and told him that it was for Rab losing his eye a couple of days ago. Jim's guts were in some mess; there was blood everywhere. Both his small and large intestines, as well as his spleen, were punctured. Jim was rushed to Stirling Royal Infirmary and they performed a life-saving operation on him. Afterwards, Jim stayed in hospital with a colostomy bag.

However, after he had recovered sufficiently, Jim made good his escape from the hospital and went on the run in Glasgow. He ran out of money after a few weeks and turned to theft. He robbed a betting shop and a bingo hall – where he got over £14,000 – but his freedom was short-lived. The coppers soon got him.

He was brought back to jail, went on trial and received an extra fifteen years on top of his life sentence. Jim is currently in the top hall up in Perth Prison, hoping to get up to the top end where all the lifers have to go to do work experience and then train for freedom. I wish him all the very best. I like the man and he has not had an easy sentence, far from it. Respect Jim 'Forty-niner' Williamson. Your little pal, Jimmy Boy H.

JOHN CROLL

John is a total wizard when it comes to making keys, sawing bars or digging tunnels. He was serving a twelve-year sentence when he robbed a bank while out on weekend leave from Noranside open prison. He was caught and sentenced to life in prison with a fourteen-year tariff. He has been inside for going on sixteen or seventeen years now and for fifteen of those years, John has done nothing but plot his next escape bid.

His most famous escape bid to date must have been the time when he and Joe Steele, one of the Ice-Cream Wars Pair who was wrongly convicted along with Thomas Campbell, tried to walk out of the front gates of Perth Prison.

But first, for those of you not familiar with the Ice-Cream Wars, here is a shortened version of what happened when the so-called war came to a head on the night of 16 April 1984. Six members of one family, including an eighteen-month-old baby, were burned to death when rival ice-cream van operators set their house on fire. Minor skirmishes had been going on for years, as rival vans 'poached' on each others' rounds.

No one actually owned the rights to these runs but, by virtue of longevity of usage, ice-cream van operators laid fierce claim to their own created routes and defended them with vigour. Obviously when a new van – or a van from a different company – appeared on a 'run', tempers grew short and violence soon flared.

During the seventies and into the eighties, the violence was more verbal than physical, and few assaults, if any, took place. But more and more people saw an ice-cream van as a means to a lucrative business; new faces began to move in on what the established traders considered their personal territory – resulting in tyres being slashed and bricks being hurled through the windscreens of 'poaching' vans.

In September 1983, the battle for control of these ice-cream routes erupted into all-out war and serious violence was inflicted. At Garthamlock, an expansive housing scheme in the northeast of Glasgow, the battle for the more lucrative routes witnessed violence that escalated out of control.

On 29 September that year, two young men attacked a rival ice-cream van with shotguns and smashed its windows. These two men were alleged to have been Joseph Steele and Thomas Campbell.

On the same night, two gunmen approached John Brady while he was working from his van, but he drove off before they could do anything. The following day, Andrew Doyle and James Lockhart grew afraid when they realised that four armed men in a car were trailing their van.

During the month of October, there were several attacks on vans, building up to 27 October when, in one night, three vans operated by the Marchetti ice-cream company were attacked by a gang of hammer-wielding youths in Garthamlock.

The following day, the Marchetti company secretary, Archie McDougall, received an anonymous phone call warning him to get his vans out of the scheme. Towards the end of 1983, ambush attacks on ice-cream vans were so commonplace that the drivers stopped reporting them to the police.

On the night of 1 February 1984, ice-cream rivals – it was alleged that Thomas Campbell and Joseph Steele led them – decided on a new course of action.

Late that night in the Balmore industrial estate, the burglar alarm went off in the Marchetti ice-cream company's building. When the police investigated, they found that an ominous-looking hole had been cut in the asbestos-covered roof and that petrol had been poured into the building. On further investigation, it was found that an attempt had been made to ignite the petrol by the rather clever means of lowering a piece of burning cloth, but it had obviously failed.

The same night, and undeterred by their failure on the industrial estate, the arsonists struck again. This time, though, the building and vans inside were badly damaged. Campbell and Steele were later charged with this arson attack, but were found to be not guilty.

The vans were soon back in competition, but not without further trouble. On 29 February, Andrew Doyle, known as 'Fat Boy', was the victim of an attack. Two shots were fired through the windscreen of his van.

Some time later, Thomas Campbell would be charged with the attempted murder of Doyle and a fifteen-year-old girl who was working in the van at the time of the attack. Another girl, a customer, was assaulted as she stood waiting to be served and was told to move away.

Over the next few weeks, several more attacks were aimed at the Marchetti vans, one of the most serious occurring on 30 March, when a driver, John Shepherd, was stabbed in the head and had his van wrecked.

A few nights later, Andrew Doyle was attacked outside his house at 29 Bankhead Street and was warned off. Four men – Thomas Campbell, Joseph Steele, Thomas Gray and Gary Moore – were arrested for the assault, but no evidence could be produced against them and they were released without charge.

On 11 and 12 April, two ice-cream vans were attacked; one of the owners, a woman called Irene Mitchell, was struck on the head with a brick. Things seemed to be reaching a state of heightened violence; each attack seemed to be worse than the last and things culminated on the night of 16 April, when the Ice-Cream War ended in a terrifying criminal action that would shock and horrify the nation.

The Doyle family, including Andrew, lived in the top flat of 29 Bankhead Street, Garthamlock, a modern, three-storey tenement. Access to their house was gained from a common stairway, with the front doors opening onto verandas.

Early in the morning of 16 April 1984, two shadowy figures mounted the stairs to the top flat and poured petrol into an outside coal cellar, next to the front door of the house. Without conscience, the arsonists set the petrol alight, crept back down the stairs to the street and disappeared into the dead of night, obviously satisfied that the fright this would give the family would persuade them to ply their trade elsewhere.

What the fire-starters did not know was that there was a stack of spare tyres inside the coal cellar – which subsequently caught fire. Dense, black smoke billowed from the bunker and soon found its way into the house. Out of the eight people who were staying there that night, six were to die from burning and smoke inhalation, including the eighteen-month-old baby.

The public and police alike were stunned at the terrible nature of the crime and, for a time, the police did not seem to be making much progress in the case. In an attempt to find the arsonists, fifty police officers, detectives and uniformed, were deployed and over 4,000 statements were taken from the public. Even so, they uncovered no incriminating evidence; they had hit a brick wall.

The police eventually carried their enquiries into the remand wing of Barlinnie Prison. Of course, there would be plenty of people there who would be eager and willing informants vying to barter information in exchange for winning bail. Barlinnie is a well known sounding board for criminal gossip, and it was there that the police found exactly what they were looking for.

William McDonald Love, an associate of Thomas Campbell and Joseph Steele, was on remand for having committed an armed robbery in a scrap-metal yard in the Gorbals. He told detectives that he had information about the fire and asked to speak to the detective in charge of the investigation.

Love had failed time after time to win bail and had been on remand for several weeks. So, on 20 March 1985, Detective Superintendent Norman Walker went to the remand wing of the prison to interview him. A deal was struck and, on 9 May, Love was brought in front of a sheriff where he made a statement saying that he had heard Thomas Campbell and Joseph Steele plotting to light a fire at the Doyle house 'to give them a fright'. Not surprisingly, after having made his statement, Love made another application for bail: this time it was granted unopposed.

Shortly after taking Love's 'evidence', detectives arrested Thomas Campbell and Joseph Steele and charged them, along with others, with a catalogue of sixteen offences, including conspiracy to assault and rob, presenting shotguns, wilful fire-raising and, finally, the murder of the Doyle family at 29 Bankhead Street, Garthamlock.

The mainstay of the evidence against them was the statement made by Love; another man, Joseph Granger, supported this evidence. Both of these men, one-time associates of Thomas Campbell and Joseph Steele, told police how they had heard the accused plotting to commit attacks upon ice-cream vans, the fire attack on the Marchetti building and assaults on people who worked for the Marchetti company. However, other than the statements made by Love and Granger, there was no real evidence that either Campbell or Steele had been anywhere near Bankhead Street on the night of the murders. At the trial, the police presented verbal statements such as: 'I thought you would've been here before this,' and 'The fire at the Fat Boy's was only meant to be a frightener', and 'It wasn't me who lit the match', all of which had allegedly been made by either Campbell or Steele at the time of their arrest.

Irrespective of the lack of hard evidence, the jury chose to believe the statements made by Love and Granger and the alleged verbal evidence presented by the police. At the end of the trial, both men were found guilty of the murders and sentenced to life imprisonment.

Throughout their incarceration, both men continued the fight to prove their innocence. William Macdonald Love has subsequently gone on record to state that his statement was a pack of lies. In fact, it has even been proven that, on the date when he was supposed to have overheard Campbell and Steele talking, Love was elsewhere.

Joseph Steele made several escapes during his sentence and each time he made a very public protest about his innocence and demanded an inquiry. He once climbed onto the roof of his mother's house after escaping from a prison escort on a home visit. As mentioned, another time he tied himself to a crane outside Barlinnie Prison and, on one memorable occasion, he super-glued himself to the gates of Buckingham Palace.

Thomas Campbell ended up in the Barlinnie special unit alongside Jimmy Boyle and carried out his campaign to get the case reopened from there. In 1992, through a ruling by European Court of Human Rights, he won new rights for prisoners regarding their legal mail, which prevented the authorities from opening correspondence between a lawyer and a client. There was a continuous demand from the public for an appeal to be heard and many demonstrations were held, both outside prisons and on the streets of Glasgow, to try and get the case reopened.

Finally, after twelve years of campaigning, and based mainly on Love's repeated admissions that he lied to the police in his statement, Thomas Campbell and Joseph Steele were given leave to appeal and were released on bail pending the hearing.

It came as a great shock to everyone when, after more than a year of freedom – during which Campbell operated an ice-cream run – the appeal judges ruled that Love's retraction was not valid, as he was confused about the dates when he claimed to have overheard the conversation. However, that is history. They both eventually won their release.

I will now tell you about how Joe and John Croll tried to escape by walking through the gates of Perth Prison. John was dressed up as one of the reception screws, with a white jacket over the black trousers he had on. Joe, on the other hand, wasn't dressed up at all; he just had the prison's standard-issue donkey jacket on. John and Joe needed a distraction so that they could make good their escape, so all the prisoners refused to go behind their doors after the reception period finished at nine o'clock sharp. That diversion gave John and Joe enough time to slip out of the hall and along to the gate, just outside the reception.

The camera would have picked them up, but no one in the control room noticed anything out of place. Once John had opened the gate they were going great guns. One of the screws had been paid over £1,000 to slip them his keys for some two minutes; just enough time for John to make an impression of one of them.

Old John looked the part, in every way, shape and form. He even had a screw's hat on when they got to the gatehouse. John proceeded to open the door as Joe kept his eyes peeled in case any screws had tippled to them: they were still in the clear. Here they were, two lifers, with one of them dressed as a screw, in the main gatehouse of Perth's top security prison.

In desperation, John tried to open the door that would lead him and Joe out to the front desk of the jail but, for some strange reason, the key didn't seem to turn in the lock. Unbeknown to John or Joe, the locks had been changed some two days or so before they made their infamous escape bid.

Once they realised that the key wasn't going to open the lock no matter how hard they tried, they hastily retreated under the stairs in the gatehouse for some cover and safety until they could walk out along with the rest of the screws. This would have been a problem for Joe, as he still had his jail clothes on.

He tried to steal a screw's jacket that was hanging up in the office to his right, but that is when five or six screws opened the door of the gatehouse to head home after their shift in C-Hall had finished. One of the screws recognised Joe and John instantly and the game was up. Without further ado, they were escorted straight down to the seg unit and placed on strict escapees; that has never stopped Joe from escaping. It did, however, put a few spokes in old John's freedom wheels.

I met John up in the Peterhead special unit in 1997 and he was still as determined as ever to make good his chances of escaping. If John had really, really wanted to bolt from the Peterhead unit, he could have. I will not say how or why, but he knows that I know. We will keep it our little secret forever, John, eh?

I know that John has only got a short while of his fourteen-year tariff to do before he walks out of the door a free man. Incidentally, John was one of the first men in Scotland to get a mandatory life sentence under the three-strike rule. He has never murdered anyone in his fifty-three years on this planet, yet the poor old boy got a life sentence for robbing a bank... just for money. It seems that you can rape and kill young women and children and the judge will take pity on the beast responsible, but if you try to steal money from the Crown... well, that is a different story. In cases like John's, it's a story that carries a life sentence. I wish you all the best when you get out. You know I mean that from my heart, John. Shine on, you deserve a break, pal. Respect.

11

Wildcards

SHUG McGREGOR

Shug McGregor comes from Glasgow's East End. By the age of twenty-three, Shug had his own scrap yard and in Glasgow's cutthroat underworld, you don't own a scrap yard unless you are able to look after yourself properly.

Just eighteen months ago, Shug was shot three times, but the hit men who had been sent to exterminate him failed miserably. Don't get me wrong, if it wasn't for Shug's quick thinking he wouldn't be alive today. I'll write more about his would-be killers later on but, in order to maintain the underworld's code of conduct, I will not mention their names.

Shug has now moved into the security business and, along with his partner Jackie and their son and daughter, is doing very well for himself. Shug is no one's mug and would, if need be, murder anyone who tried to stand on his toes – unlike so many others in the Glasgow underworld.

I am very close to this young man: he's got a heart of gold, but never takes kindness for daftness.

TERRY CURREN

Terry Curren, known as Tel, comes from Blackhill in the East End of Glasgow. He has been on the scene for years and grew up with Paul Ferris, but in no way has his life been easy.

A man called Tam Monahan once shot Tel at point-blank range. Monahan went on to be a beast and I'm reluctant to mention the arsehole on the same page as my friend, the hard man Tel Boy.

Tel has spent his fair share of time in prison and it's a miracle that he has been out since 2001. In the early nineties, Tel got his own back on another man who had shot him. You see, there have been umpteen attempts on Terry's life by rival gangsters, but he is still living his life the only way he knows how.

Tel's son, Junior, is a big boy who has inherited all of his dad's traits. Junior works as a bouncer in the city's top nightclub, The Tunnel. I just hope he doesn't need to spend a day in prison; he shouldn't need to, as Tel has drummed it into his boy's head that prison is a mug's game – you can't make any money there or have any nice birds on your arm.

And yes, I am preaching here, and with good reason. I have spent more than eighteen years of my life in prison thinking that there was nothing better in life, until I got out, that is. My wake-up call came when I saw men who I had been in prison with, jumping about in top-of-the-range BMWs, Mercs and Land Rovers. This is the kind of thing I want to have a try at once I settle back into the community, which, fingers crossed, shouldn't be much longer.

JIM CULLEN

Jim Cullen was born in the southside of Glasgow. I met this diamond brother while I was doing time in Edinburgh's Saughton Prison back in 2001.

Since the first day we met, things between us have gone from strength to strength. Jim is more of a cash register than a hard man and he doesn't need to use violence often, but when he does blow his top, the best thing to do is to stay out of his way.

Jim has stabbed and slashed more men than he cares to remember. Recently I asked him how he started off on his journey into the Glasgow underworld. If I didn't know better, I would have thought that his upbringing came straight out of a Jeffrey Archer novel.

Jim started off with his own fruit-and-veg cart at the world-famous Barras Market in Glasgow. Before too long, he had earned enough money to open up his first shop and, within no time, he was moving in circles that he could only have dreamed about. Over the next twenty years, Jim built up a team of men who were willing to do anything for him and all sorts of doors that would never have been opened to him, suddenly flew off the hinges. Jim's name was like gold.

He is now waiting to go on trial, along with two other men, for all sorts of offences ranging from drugs and fraud to organised crime. I hope my very good friend gets a result in court for his alleged part in these offences.

Jim and the other two men have been on the cops' surveillance list for more than three years, so you can see how desperate the cops were to get their hands on them.

Jim had been rubbing shoulders with the Turks and Nigerians down in London and he also had extensive contacts with the Pakistanis in Bradford. All in all, Jim is one of Scotland's top mobsters.

For now, Jim is keeping a low profile. He has no option, as there is surveillance on him every time he leaves his semi-detached house. I hope you get off at court, big chap, as you haven't done anything wrong. We are all 100 per cent behind you, as is your lawyer.

Despite the fact that he is one of Scotland's top criminals, most people in Scotland would walk straight by him without taking a second glance. That is how good he is at his job. God bless you, mate.

GORDON FLETT

Gordon Flett is currently living in Aberdeen. He has just finished his third six-year sentence, back to back, for drug dealing in the class-A drug, heroin. This man has travelled around the world in a luxury camper van that he had custom-built. One newspaper reported that he had made over £1.2 million in cash from his run, selling drugs, so you can see that he must have run his part of Aberdeen with a rod of iron.

Gordon's pal, Thomas Pirry, was his muscle in Aberdeen. Thomas Pirry's name meant violence, at the top end of the scale. This meant that Gordon didn't need to turn to violence very often; all he had to do was snap his fingers and a problem was dealt with that day. However, things are now catching up with him. When he got out, everything had changed. I know this from first-hand experience, as I went to stay with him when I got out of prison. It just shows you that nobody is untouchable.

Gordon tried to get back into the drugs trade, but found it difficult. Drugs are a young man's game, nowadays.

DICKY PARVIN

Dicky Parvin comes from Wishaw, in the heart of Lanarkshire. This barrel-chested man has been in more violent fights and shooting incidents than any other man in Lanarkshire. I know that Dicky was friends with the Murdocks, but things between them soon went pear-shaped. So much so, that the guns soon came out and there were umpteen reported shootings – tit for tat, against each other.

The Murdocks wouldn't let things lie, so Dicky and some of his brothers took their disagreements to a different level. By this, I mean hand grenades and sub-machineguns.

Thankfully, they were never used, but they were there if needed. Dicky is currently finishing off yet another eight-year sentence for money lending... at least that is what the cops and Crown prosecutors said.

As ever, this very tough old man laughed in the judge's face when he sent him down. Dicky's two sons are now as violent and as dangerous as their old man. I would like to thank Dicky, personally, for his friendship and help while I was inside.

ARCHIE STEIN

Archie Stein is a top-of-the-range hard-man gangster, who originally came from Glasgow, but like so many other men who were released from Perth Prison, stayed and found a house in this lovely picture-postcard city.

After he had completed his life sentence and was released back into society, he had Perth to himself in no time and no one would go up against him. Within three years of being set free, Archie had made enough money to pull out of the underworld and settle down with his lovely wife.

She is now unwell, but to this hard man's credit, he has stood by her and tends to her every need. Most other hard bastards would have neither the courage nor the loyalty to look after their sick wives. Most of them would want to keep on living the high life, going from one woman to the next. I would just like to commend you, Archie, for what you have done since you were released from prison. So many others would have run a mile from that kind of thing.

THE McALLISTER BROTHERS

Jason and Derrick McAllister come from the northeast of Scotland and are originally of traveller stock. These two brothers saw a gap in the drugs trade in Aberdeen and took their chance. Before too long, the whole city was under their control and it was reported in the papers that the brothers made in the region of £2.5 million from their drugs empire.

They imported top-of-the-range motors from Europe with top-grade heroin worth hundreds of thousands of pounds hidden inside the door panels.

However, it didn't take too long for the city's grasses and prostitutes to run to the cops to spill their guts about the brothers' business. If that wasn't bad enough, their own brother, out of spite, walked straight into a police station and told the sergeant at the desk what his two younger brothers were up to.

The third brother had originally been asked to come on board, but he didn't. However, once he had seen how easy it was for his brothers, he wanted in on the business. By that stage, though, there was no room for him, so he ran to the cops and helped bring his own brothers down. They got twenty-two years' imprisonment between them. Their sentence was probably fair; Jason and Derrick tortured people who didn't pay their drug debts back. When you consider that these two brothers weighed 17st and 19st, you can imagine the punishment beatings that they dished out to people in prison. However, I found them both very pleasant indeed.

DON AND PIZZA FRATTI

Don and Pizza Fratti are a couple of very well-known hoods from the East End of Glasgow and have appeared in court for umpteen shootings and drugs charges. The two brothers are related to Mick Healy, who is the only man in the history of the Scottish penal system to have escaped from Shotts maximum-security prison in the back of a butcher's van.

Don and Pizza have been under the spotlight of Baird Street's CID division for some years now. If you are anyone in the rough, cut-throat Glasgow underworld, then you will know these two, dirty, game, hard bastards. The brothers are going from strength to strength in the underworld, where, without a doubt, they wield a considerable amount of power.

EPILOGUE

Well, another fine mess I am in. It's March 2006 and here I am back behind bars in HMP Barlinnie! Another stitch-up is what I say. My freedom lasted for a few months, during which time I had tried to turn my life around. I had secured the deposit for a bedsit, secured a little pin money from a job and was setting about turning my hopes of becoming a full-time writer into a reality. I had already finalised this book and was working on six other titles, two of which have been accepted for publication.

What happened? I was standing in the wrong place at the wrong time. All will come out in the wash, as they say. So, just for the moment, my chin is up and I will be working on regaining my freedom. In the meantime, remember what you have read here – and do your best to avoid Scotland's hard bastards.

Your pal, Jimmy Boy Holland.

ACKNOWLEDGEMENTS

I would like to give special thanks to the following people for standing by me through the time I lay in solitary. Firstly, my Auntie Rose and my two little cousins, Lizzy and Lynne. Also Davie and Lee, young Colette for always being kind to me when I phoned my lawyer's office, also my lawyer Jack Brown. My QC, George Gebbie, my big friend Alan and his family Steph and Sharon, my old mam Liz and my brother Rubin. Finally, but no means least, a special thanks to Linda and Scott for showing me their love and kindness, I couldn't have done this without you all. Steve you are a top man, I have nothing but love in my heart for you.

FURTHER READING

Other titles by Stephen Richards available from Blake Publishing.

Insanity: My Mad Life (Paperback & Hardback)
Charles Bronson with Stephen Richards
ISBN: 1844540308
Charles Bronson is the most feared and the most notorious convict in the prison system. Renowned for serial hostage-taking and his rooftop sieges, he is a legend in his own lifetime. Yet behind the crime and the craziness, there is a great deal more to Charlie.

The Krays and Me (Hardback)
Charles Bronson with Stephen Richards
ISBN: 1844540421
'Since Ronnie and Reggie died, all I've heard is a load of bollocks! Reggie shot my cat; Ronnie stabbed my Uncle Bert seventy-five times; Reggie ran over my hamster; I'm

Ronnie's son; I'm Reggie's daughter. Gutless maggots spreading rumours with their sham stories for sale.'

The Good Prison Guide (Hardback)
Charles Bronson with Stephen Richards
ISBN: 1844540227
Charlie Bronson has taken his twenty-four years' experience of prison dwelling and condensed it into one handy and comprehensive volume. Moved regularly around the prisons of the British Isles, he has sampled all that prison life has to offer, taking in both the historic and pre-historic buildings that comprise Britain's infamous prison system. It's all in here, from the correct way to brew vintage prison 'hooch' and how to keep the screws from finding it, to the indispensable culinary methods required to make prison food edible.

The Lost Girl (Hardback & Paperback)
Caroline Roberts with Stephen Richards
ISBN: 1843581485
Caroline Roberts is a survivor. Just sixteen years old when she was hitchhiking home from a weekend away with her boyfriend, she was picked up by two of the most twisted and dangerous people in the country, names that would, years later, become synonymous with pure evil: Fred and Rose West. Unsuspecting, she took a job as a nanny to the Wests. The events that followed were to scar her for the rest of her life.

It's Criminal (Hardback)
ISBN: 1844540596
James Crosbie with Stephen Richards
Once dubbed 'the most dangerous man in Scotland' and notorious for his dangerous bank raids, James Crosbie knew no bounds or fear when it came to getting what he wanted. Although he has tried to 'go straight' many times, the temptation of scoring that one great haul has been too great to keep him from a life of crime. This is his extraordinary story.

Born to Fight (Hardback)
Richy Horsley with Stephen Richards
ISBN: 1844540960
There are few men tougher than Richy Horsley. Boxer, street fighter and bouncer, Crazy Horse, as he is better known, is part of the underbelly of the hard man scene. So tough is he, that he has even accepted a challenge from Britain's most dangerous prisoner, Charles Bronson, to be his first boxing opponent upon Bronson's eventual release from prison. As a young man, he channeled his rage into boxing and he became one of the toughest fighters in the land.

Street Warrior (Hardback)
Malcolm Price with Stephen Richards
ISBN: 1904034632
'They surround me and get me in a headlock. Everyone gets a boot in. So I lean down and twist the guy's legs. He lets go and I grab a glass and slice him across the face. A

piece of flesh goes flying across the room. "Who else wants a visit to the hospital?" I yell as everything kicks off...' Malcolm Price was born to fight. As a child his father made him go and box in the gym. At first he didn't want to, but he soon found he knew how to punch and it wasn't long before 'Pricey' had become a feared and respected figure.

Crash 'n' Carry (Paperback)
Stephen Richards
ISBN: 1844541061
Crash 'n' Carry is the astonishing true story of the rise and rise of the ramraider. In this startling investigation, top true crime writer Steve Richards reveals the shocking truth. He shows that far from being just petty chancers, ramraiders are in fact part of highly organised gangs, masterminded by career criminals who systematically select and raid their targets. One such gang got away with £100 million of stolen goods in a daring heist that shocked the international crime-fighting community.

The Taxman (Hardback)
Brian Cockerill with Stephen Richards
ISBN: 1844541347
Over the last two decades, Teesside's Brian Cockerill has ruled his world with an iron fist and dished out instant justice to the scum drug dealers. Using nothing but his hands as weapons, he has patrolled the streets, clubs and raves of Britain in order to keep order and to 'tax' those whose ill-gotten gains he sees fit to take a share of. Drug

dealers and shady club promoters everywhere know that if The Taxman is in town, it's time to pay up or get out. They all know of the appalling violence that this man can exert on his enemies and of the incredible presence of body and mind that he possesses.

Lost in Care (Hardback)
Jimmy Holland with Stephen Richards
ISBN: 1844541614
Jimmy Holland was born into a family suffering at the hands of their drunk and abusive father. At the age of just two weeks, he was placed into care. And so began a life lived in a constantly changing environment of homes, authorities and institutions. Let down and frequently abused, it wasn't long before Jimmy strayed onto the wrong side of the tracks and the mould for a problem child was set. He quickly turned from substance abuse to drug use and, in turn, to crime – his only means of an escape. An inevitable lifetime of crime faced him and he soon became associated with the ringleaders of an infamous gang responsible for prison riots and hostage taking. A heartfelt, shocking and despairing insight into life as a state-raised boy, *Lost in Care* is the heart-rending tale of a man who has lost his childhood and who has also lost his way.

Viv Graham: Britain's Most Feared Gangster
(Paperback)
Stephen Richards
ISBN: 1844541274

Viv Graham's name means many things to many people. A legend in his own lifetime, he worked his way to the very top of the North East's criminal elite until his iron grip on its activities extended to the darkest corner of the underworld. The mere mention of his name would strike dread into the hearts of his enemies and all knew that, if Viv was after you, then hell was coming with him. His frightening capacity for extreme violence was never questioned, and his size and ability to fight enabled him to exert a huge influence on those around him – but he also had a reputation as a hard man with a heart of gold who looked after those that looked after each other. In this frank and astonishing book, Stephen Richards peels away the tissue of lies surrounding the life and death of Viv Graham and, using information from over 350 of Viv's closest friends and family associates, he finally tells the brutal and tragic stories of one of gangland's greatest heroes.

Fight to the Death: Viv Graham and Lee Duffy –
Too Hard to Live, Too Young to Die (Paperback)
Stephen Richards
ISBN: 1844542459

Viv Graham and Lee Duffy led parallel lives as pub and club enforcers, raging their gangland turf wars with a fierce frenzy of brutality and unremitting cruelty. This frank and astonishing book by underworld authority Stephen Richards is a riveting double portrait of two of the North East's most feared men whose bloody rivalry was cut short when they each met horrifically violent ends. With a frightening capacity for extreme violence, Tyneside protection hard man Viv struck fear into the hearts of his enemies, yet his benevolence to local charities and schemes to keep kids away from drugs and crime was well known – any patch that Viv protected was guaranteed to be free of both. He was the ultimate maverick trouble-shooter. Teeside drugs enforcer Lee Duffy had half his foot shot off in an assassination attempt and his skull beaten with a crowbar, but his streetwise instinct was unmatched. With unprecedented access to friends, family and associates, Stephen Richards dispels many of the myths surrounding these legendary figures.

Hailey's Story (Hardback)
Hailey Giblin with Stephen Richards
ISBN: 1844541916
Hailey Giblin was just eleven years old when she had the misfortune of meeting Ian Huntley, the Soham murderer. He brutally assaulted her and threatened to kill her if she told anyone what he had done. She eventually told her mother of her ordeal. Huntley was questioned, but released without charge due to a lack of evidence. When Hailey learned of the arrest of Huntley for the Soham murders, her nightmare came flooding back to her. In this heart-rending book, Hailey tells her story in her own

words. She bravely tells how, despite having been robbed of her childhood, she has fought to recover from this tragic event.

Psycho Steve (Hardback)
Stephen Moyle with Stephen Richards
ISBN: 1844542513
A decent sort of psychopath... When a £1 million construction deal starts to go pear-shaped and a London heavy mob working for the opposition ransack his house, Stephen Moyle is out for revenge. In a tale of violence and adventure via the north of England, the English Channel and Canada, Stephen recounts the events – including an audacious escape from HMP Camp Hill and a swim across the Solent – that led to a 3 and a half year jail term and his eventual sectioning.